Sketchbook Pages

Volume Two

2006 - 2009

by

Amelia Fais Harnas

Self-published in
Portland, OR

ISBN 978-0-578-02930-6

VOLUME III

FOR THE FIRST TIME IN MY LIFE,
WHEN I LOOK BEHIND ME, I AM
CAUGHT OFF GUARD BY THE
CONSIDERABLE DISTANCE TRAVELED.
THE THREE YEARS IN THIS VOLUME
SPAN TWO SKETCHBOOKS, ONE
HUNDRED FIFTY-FIVE PAGES, SIX
RESIDENCES, TWO COASTS, FOUR
COUNTRIES, AT LEAST 27,000 MILES,

THREE LANGUAGES, TWO BICYCLES,
AND A COUNTLESSLY RENEWED
RESOLUTION TO BE FEARLESS.
AINSI SOIT-IL.

05.13.09

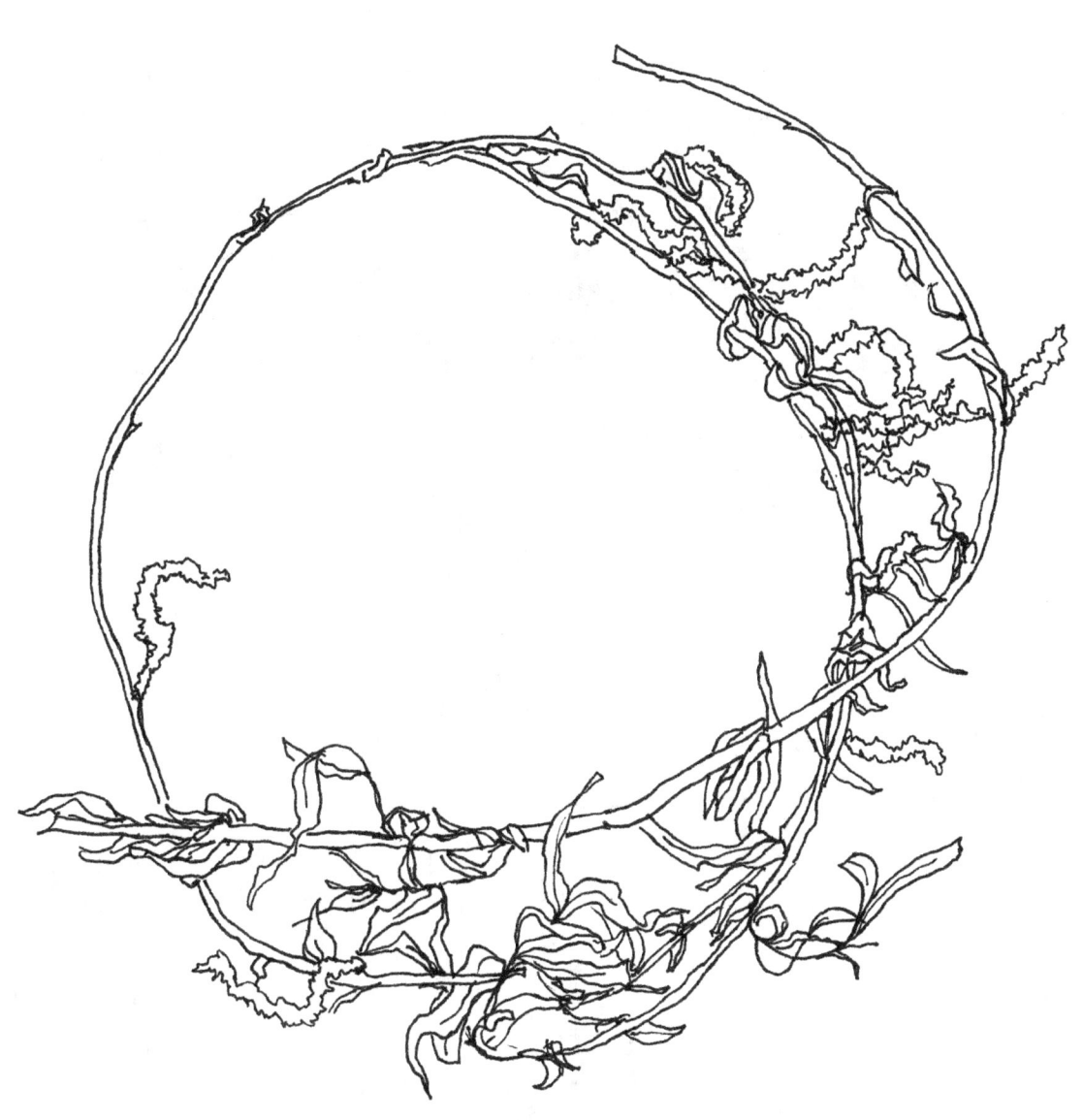

I will take your hand and we will
walk until we can't anymore we will
lie under willow trees and watch clouds
and starlings fly we will break the ties
to all that we call messes we will never
die and I will love you always...

07.21.06

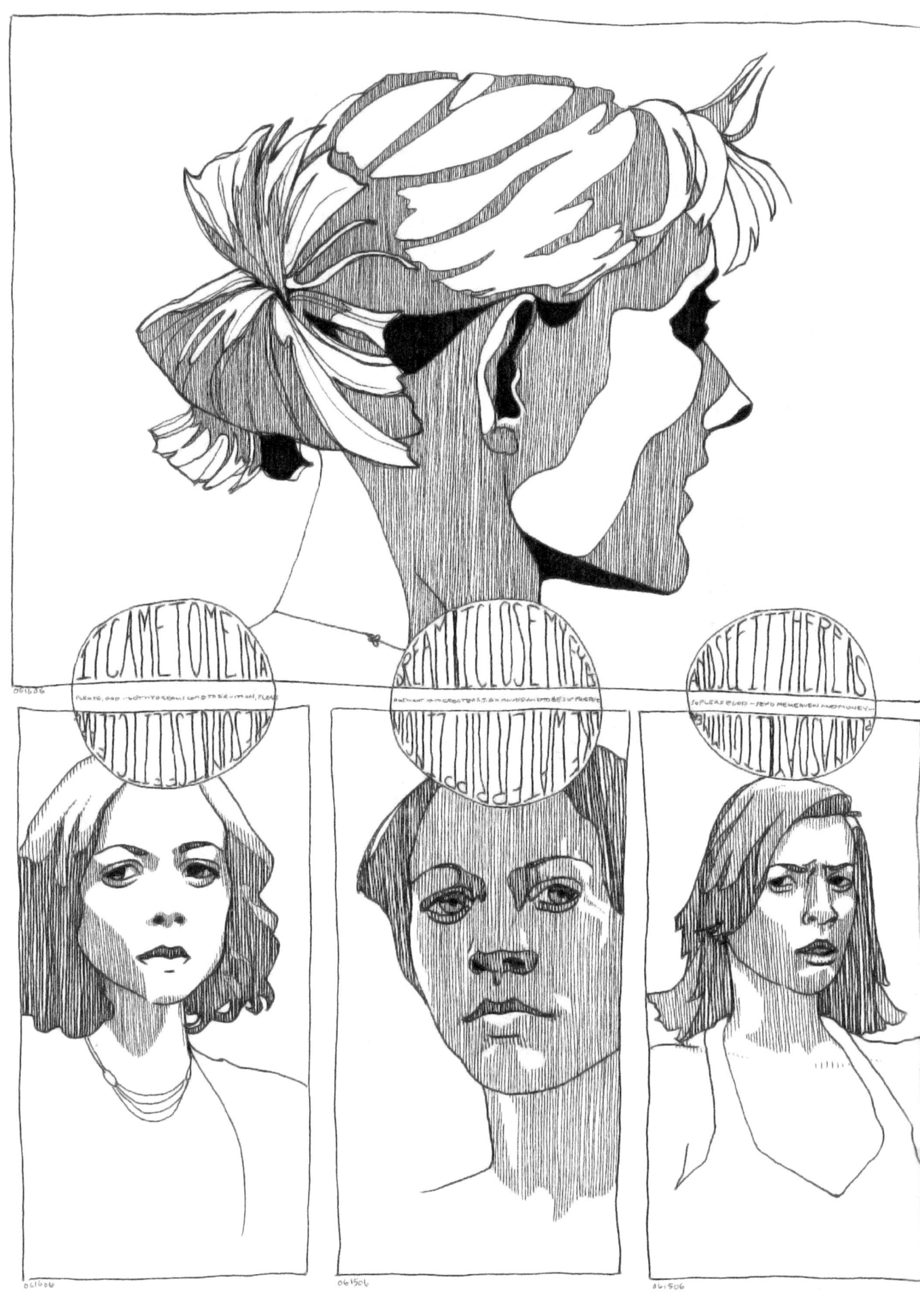

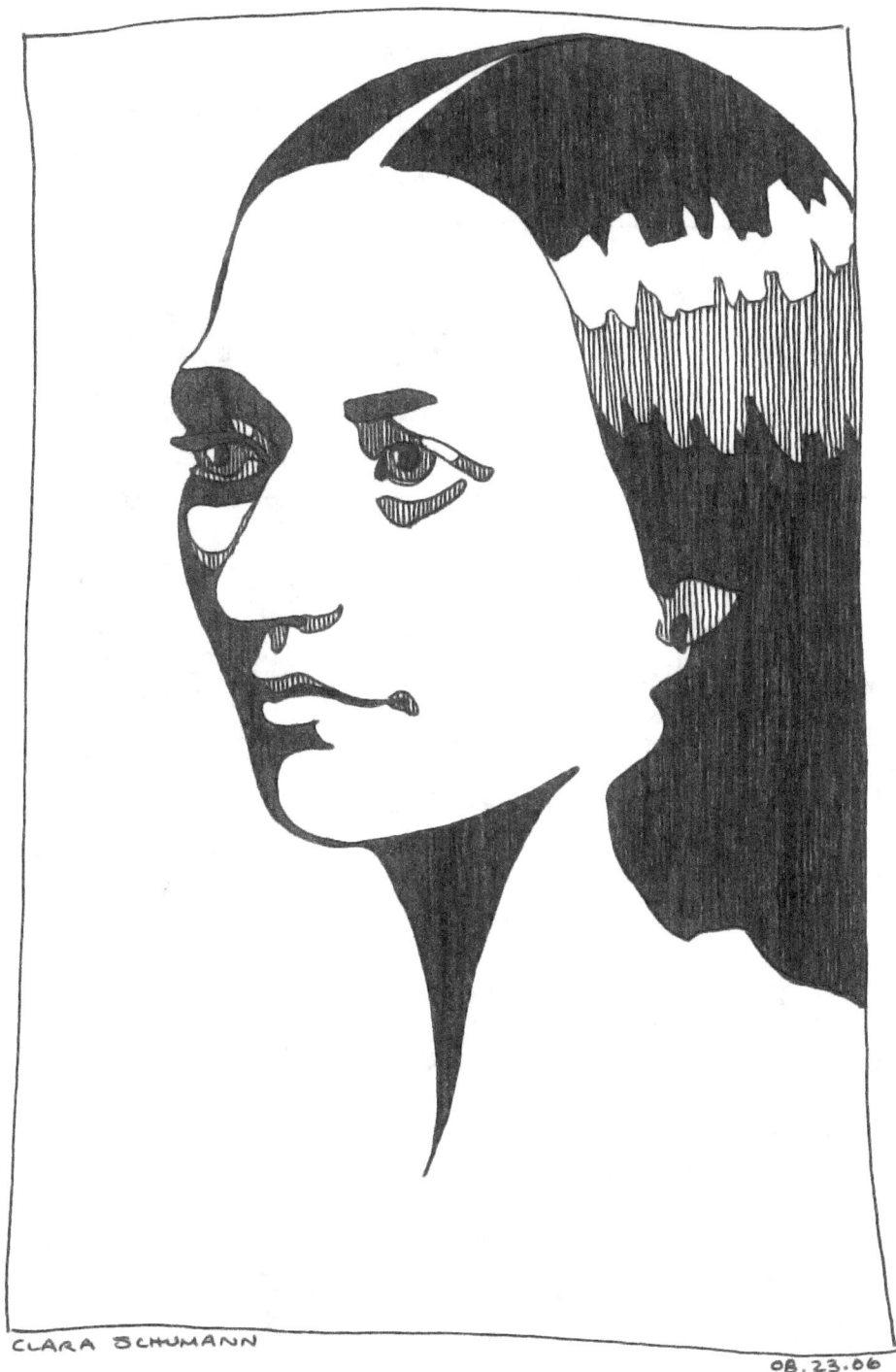

CLARA SCHUMANN

08.23.06

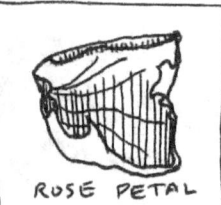
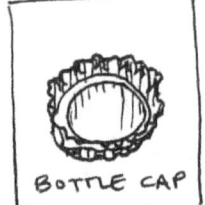
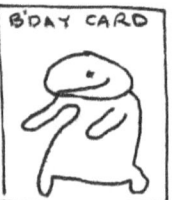

DON'T GIVE UP. IN THE END, IT'S WORTH IT.

"PERHAPS EVERYTHING TERRIBLE IS IN ITS DEEPEST BEING SOMETHING HELPLESS THAT WANTS HELP FROM US." — RAINER MARIA RILKE

ROSE PETAL

BOTTLE CAP

B'DAY CARD

08

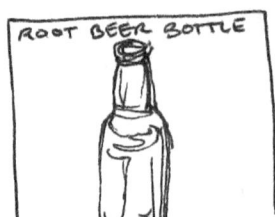
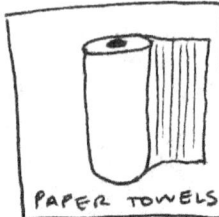
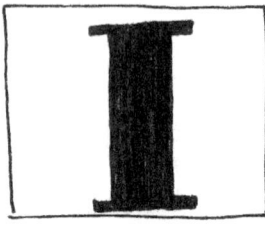
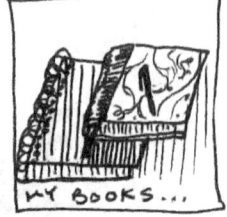
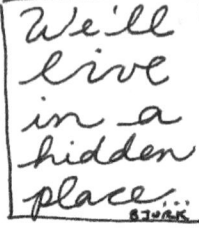

ROOT BEER BOTTLE

PAPER TOWELS

I

MY BOOKS...

We'll live in a hidden place... BJORK

25

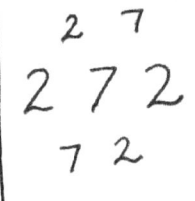
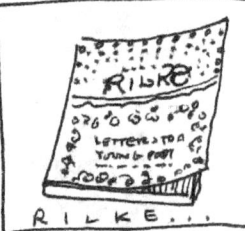
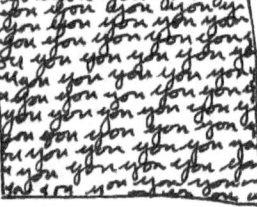
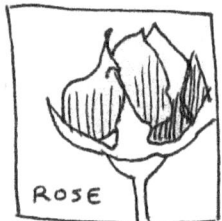

2 7
2 7 2
7 2

RILKE...

"FOR THIS REASON, IT WILL NOT CEASE TO BE DIFFICULT, BUT FOR THIS REASON TOO IT WILL NOT CEASE TO GROW. AND IF THERE IS ONE THING MORE I MUST TELL YOU, IT IS THIS:" — RMR

ROSE

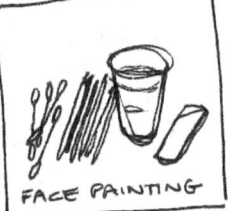
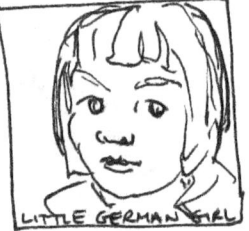
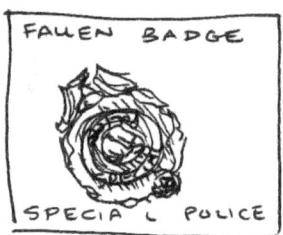
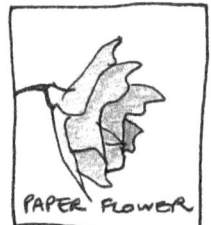

THE ODD FELLOW IN THE BASEBALL CAP WALKS IN AND SITS DOWN. DRINKS A CUP & WIPES IT CLEAN WITH HIS FINGER - LICK, LICK, LICK, LICK, LICK...

FACE PAINTING

LITTLE GERMAN GIRL

FALLEN BADGE

SPECIAL POLICE

PAPER FLOWER

08

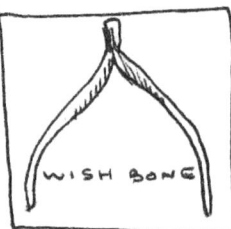
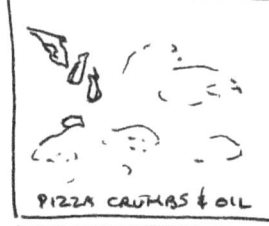
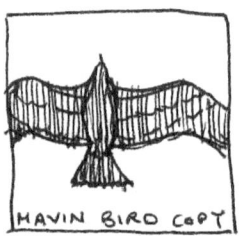

I M B O R E D

HE WANTED A PICTURE OF ME AND HIM TOGETHER. I COULD TELL THAT HE WAS A CHARACTER AND A BIT "TOUCHED." HE AWKWARDLY GROPED MY ARM AND SMILED AS THE CAMERA FLASH

WISH BONE

PIZZA CRUMBS & OIL

HAVIN BIRD COPY

26

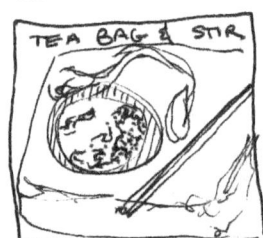
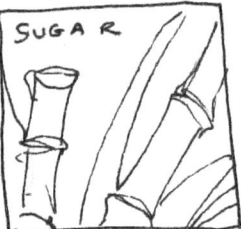
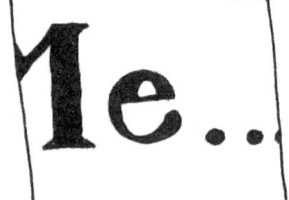
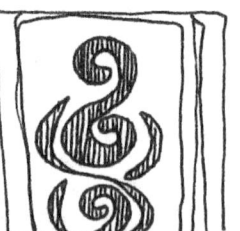

TEA BAG & STIR

SUGAR

Me...

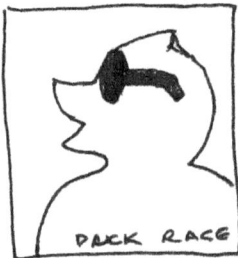
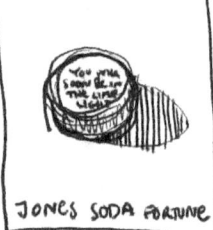
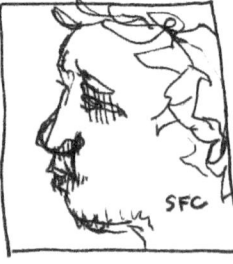

DUCK RACE

JONES SODA FORTUNE

SFC

COFFEE BAR

06

avoiding the crowds and noise, I walk along on the railroad tracks behind the parking garage my shoes sink with each step into the soft, slip-like clay and grass between the two rails. I stop to look at the dead and reddened fir tree among a grove of green. Suddenly, I am struck with the feeling someone is following me — I look behind me to see no one — but as I turn back to my path, I see writing on the brick wall of the garage. It's your name, someone had scraped it in chalk or with a soft stone on the red brick.

I just stop, staring for a long time. Funny thing is, I had a feeling it was you that was following me just then.
08.26.06

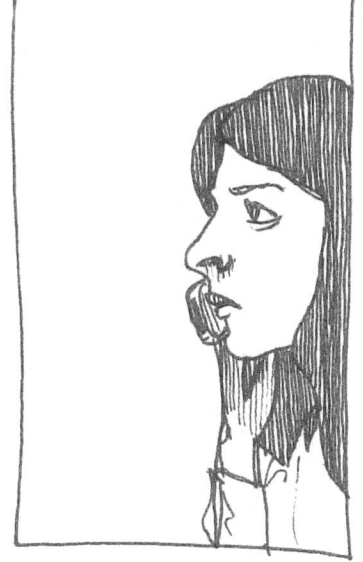

YOU MUST HAVE A WARM MOUTH... ...LIKE A FURNACE HONEY. -RHONDA S. PON

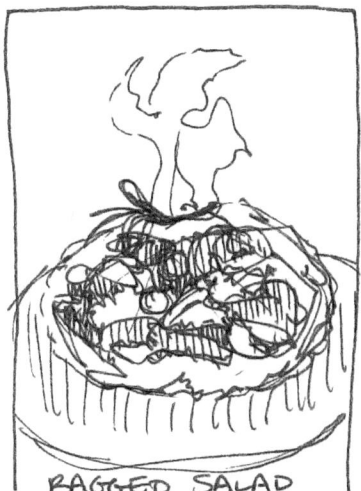

BAGGED SALAD

227 POINTS FOR BEING THE BEST TABLE OF THE NIGHT FOR JUSTIN. THAT GUY I KNOW SOMEHOW
08.27.06

WE'RE BOTH HUNGRY, SO AFTER MIKE LIGHTS A CIGARETTE WE CROSS THE STREET TWICE— AS TO AVOID THE CONSTRUCTION ON THE LOCAL COURTHOUSE AFTER THE BIG FLOOD THAT HIT IN JUNE — AND WALKED ALONG THE GREEN SQUARE. I LOOKED UP AND THERE WAS AN OLD COUNTY (OR TOWN—I FORGET WHICH) JAIL THAT A RESTAURANT HAD REMODELED. WE WENT IN AND WERE SEATED IN AN OLD JAIL CELL THAT HAD A TINY ECHO. MIKE ORDERED A GRILLED CHICKEN SANDWICH. I HAD THE TOMATO SOUP.

TIME IS ON MY SIDE, YES IT IS —TIME IS ON MY SIDE, I SAID IT IS. OH-SORRY GUYS — DIDN'T SEE YOU GUYS THERE.
08.31.06

She gave me the warmest hug—a strong embrace. She told me she had always admired me from afar, but this afternoon, a simple wave just would not do—she rushed across the street, and told me these things that must had been weighing heavily over the years. I've always known her, too. But always as a mystery.

But what always made me feel badly was that I never knew her name. Now I do...
090106

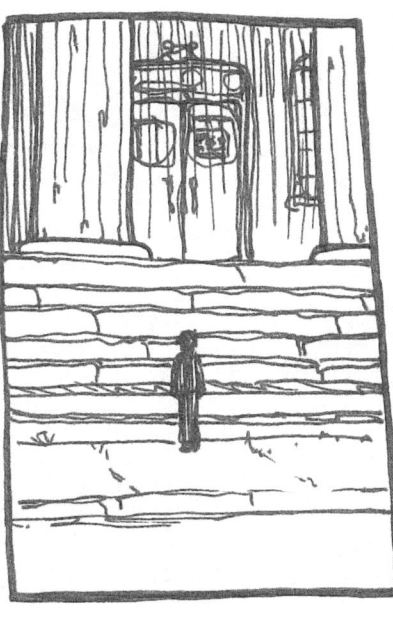

He must be ten. He's looking so reverently at the old War Memorial Library as if it were a monument. Maybe it really is.
09.01.06

"KEEP ON BEING BIG IN THIS LIFE, AMELIA"
— LISA

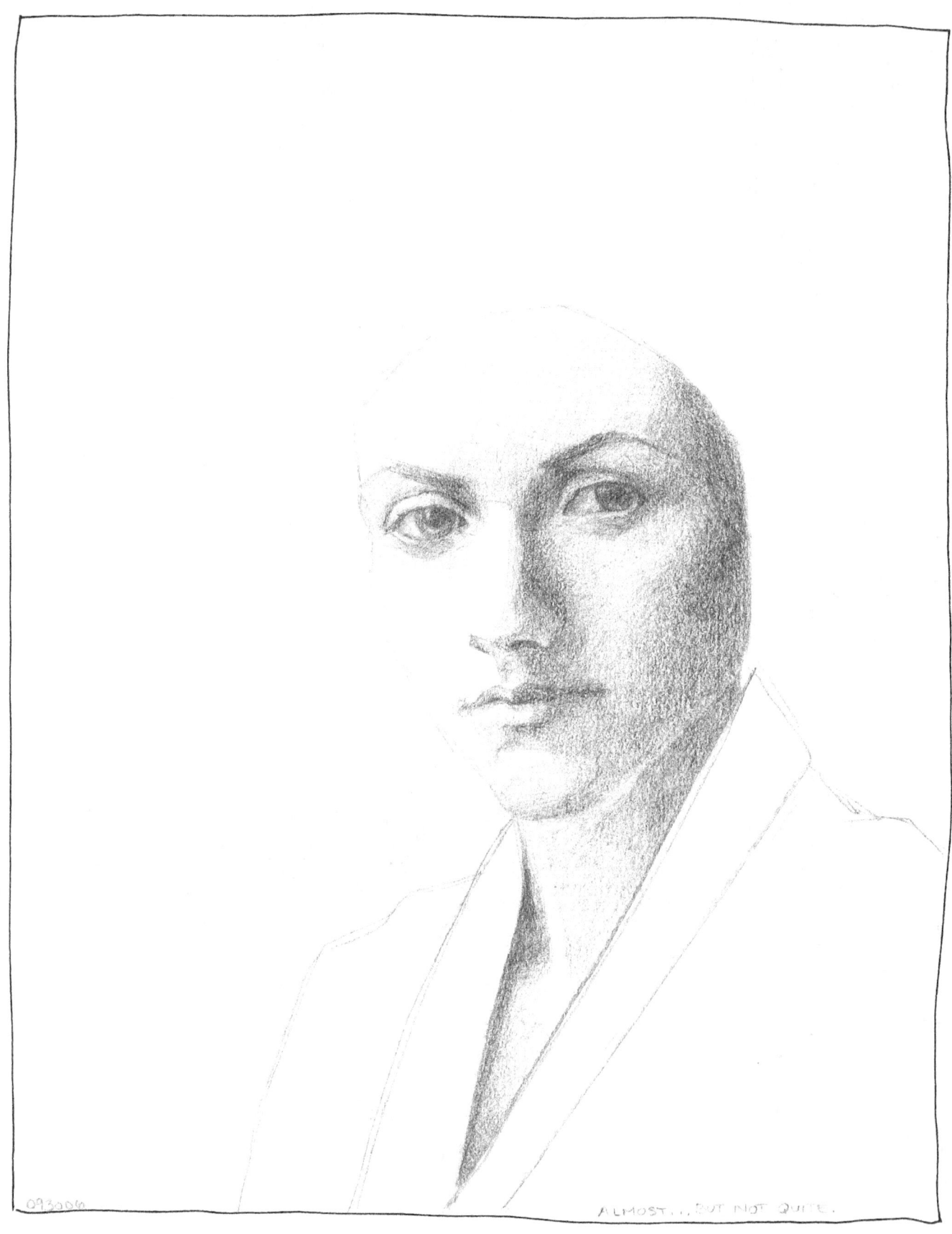

093006   ALMOST... BUT NOT QUITE.

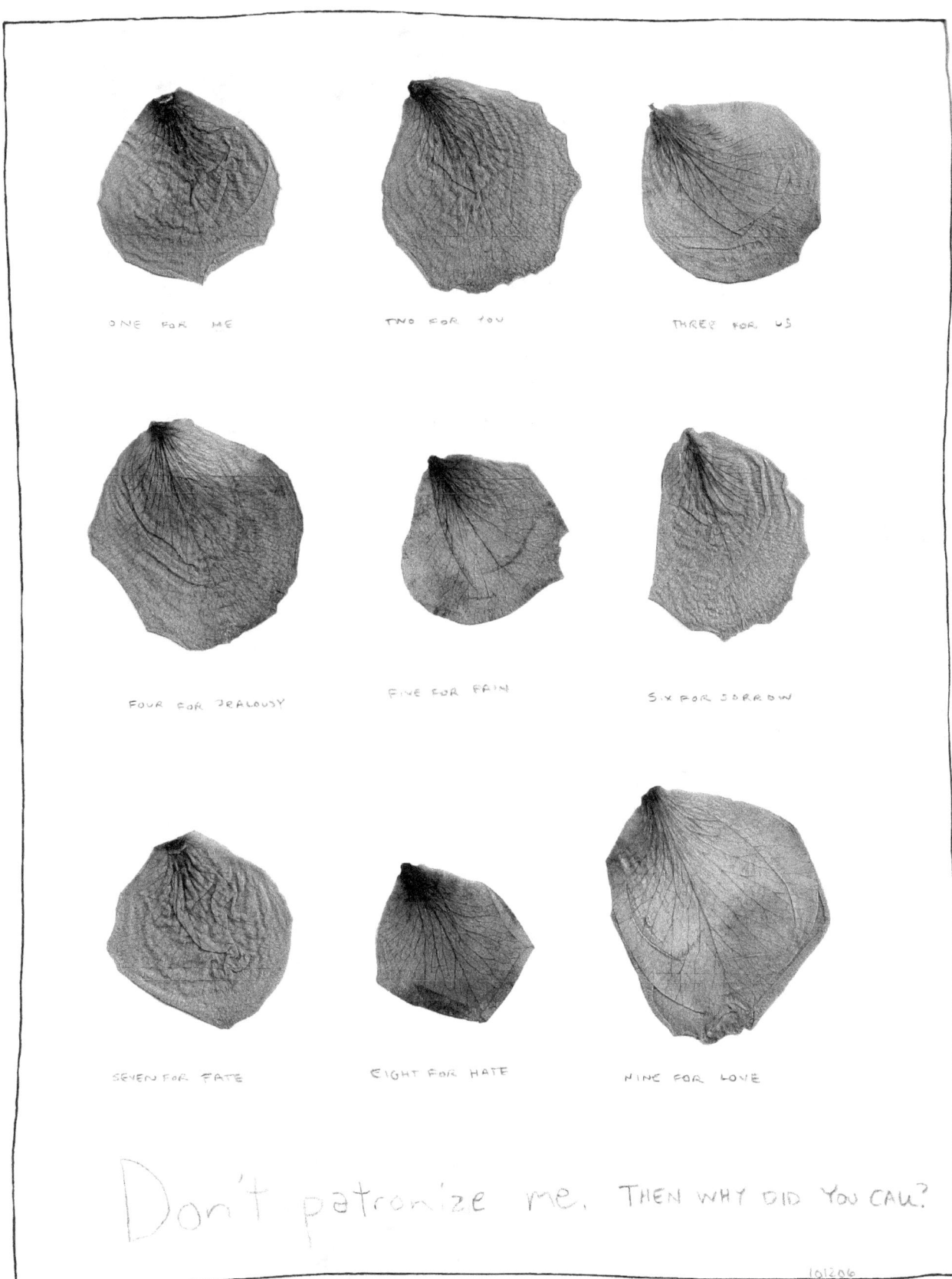

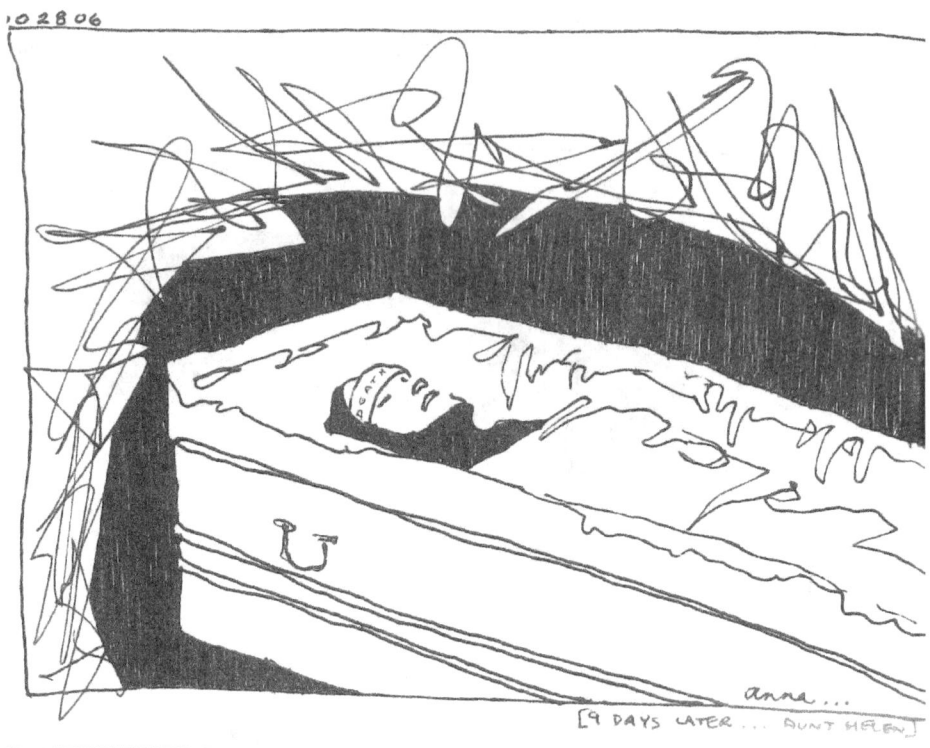

102806

anna...

[9 DAYS LATER... AUNT HELEN]

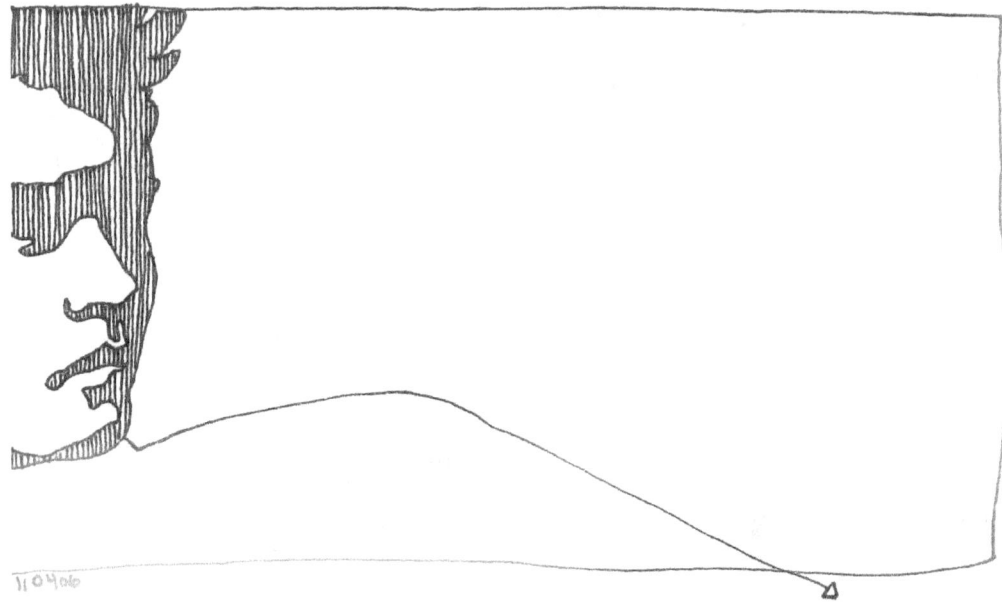

110406

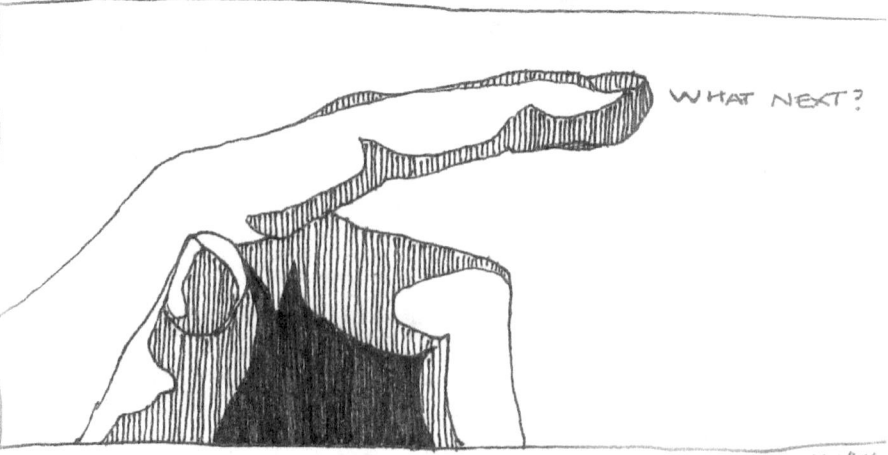

WHAT NEXT?

110406

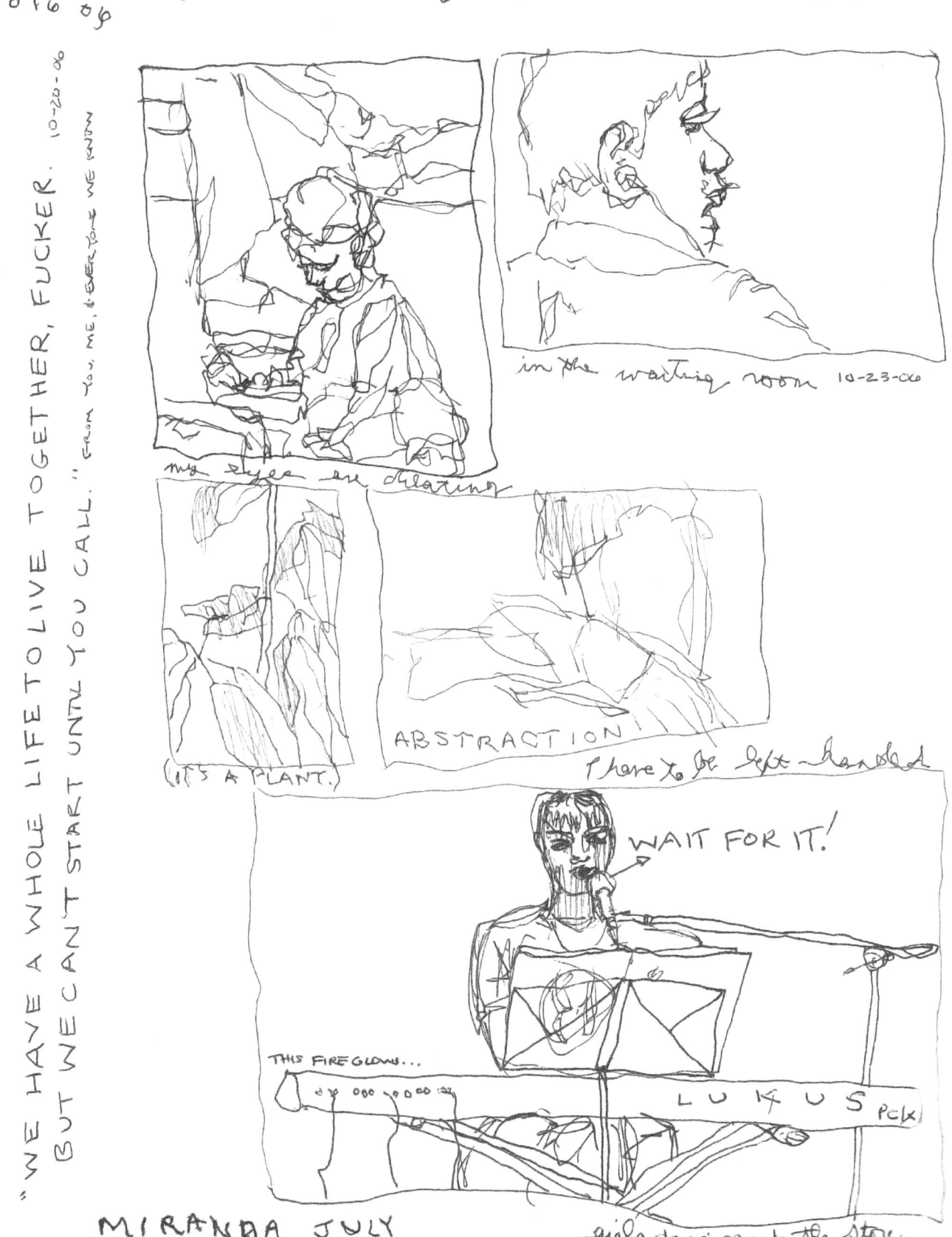

I am in the emergency room with a nasty, bloody dog bite on my right middle ~~~~ finger. 10-16-06

"WE HAVE A WHOLE LIFE TO LIVE TOGETHER, FUCKER. 10-20-06
BUT WE CAN'T START UNTIL YOU CALL." FROM YOU, ME, & EVERYONE WE KNOW

in the waiting room 10-23-06

my nurse is dilating

(IT'S A PLANT.)

ABSTRACTION

I have to be left-handed

WAIT FOR IT!

THIS FIRE GLOWS...

LUKUS PCIX

MIRANDA JULY

girls dancing at the store

11-05-06
THE DAY AFTER

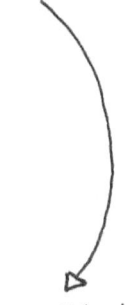

LET'S TRY THIS AGAIN — I WILL DROP A PENNY & WHERE IT
LANDS, I WILL MOVE THERE. OR IN THAT AREA...

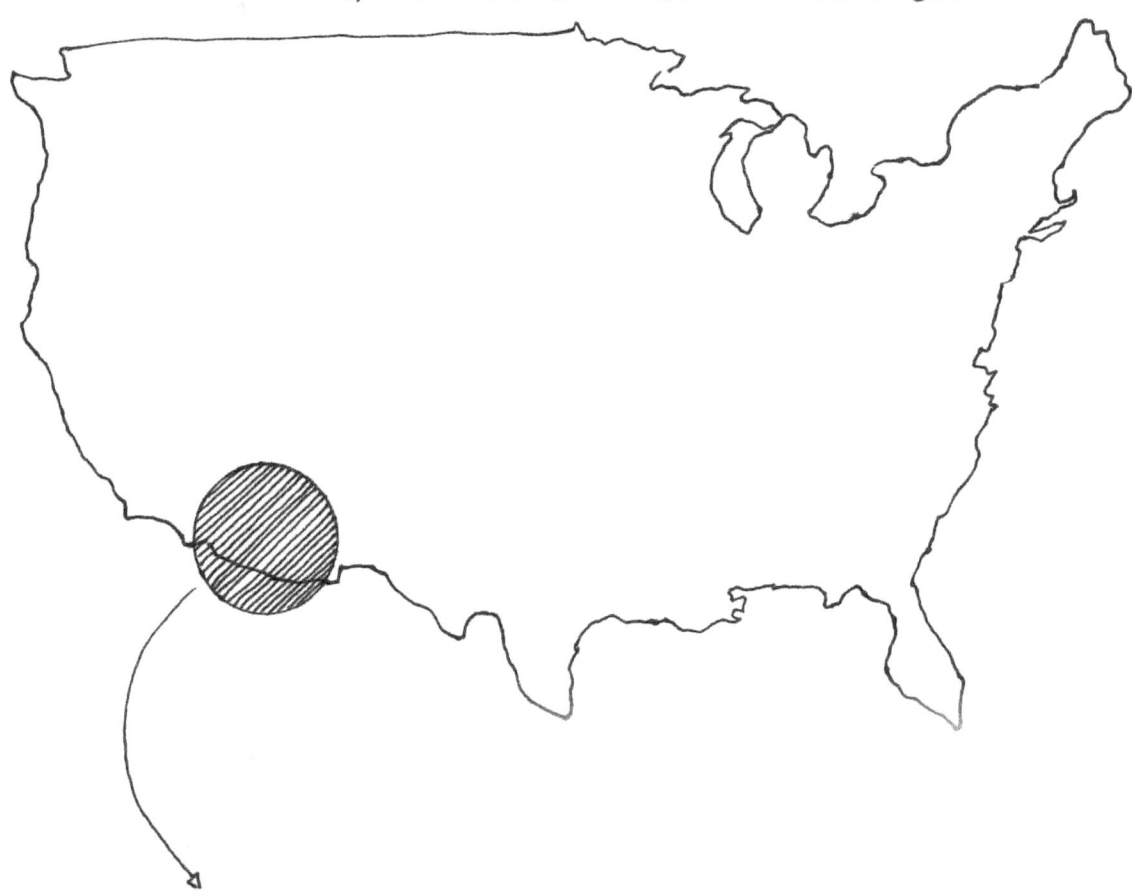

POSSIBLE PLACES IN THIS REGION:
1. PHOENIX
2. TUCSON
3. TOMBSTONE
4. SEDONA
5. FLAGSTAFF
6. GILBERT
7. MEXICO

YEAH... I DON'T THINK SO.

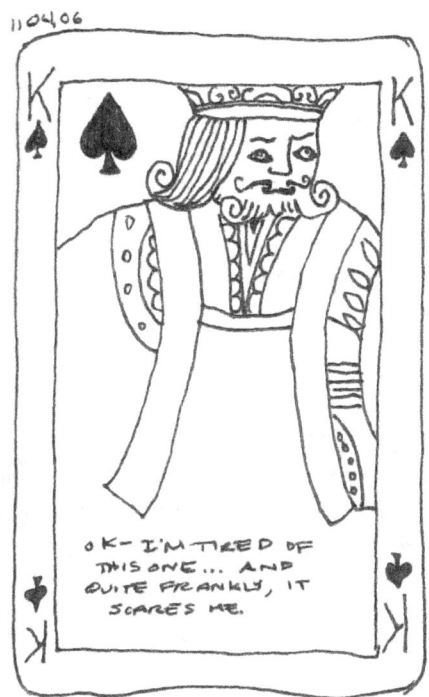

OK- I'M TIRED OF
THIS ONE... AND
QUITE FRANKLY, IT
SCARES ME.

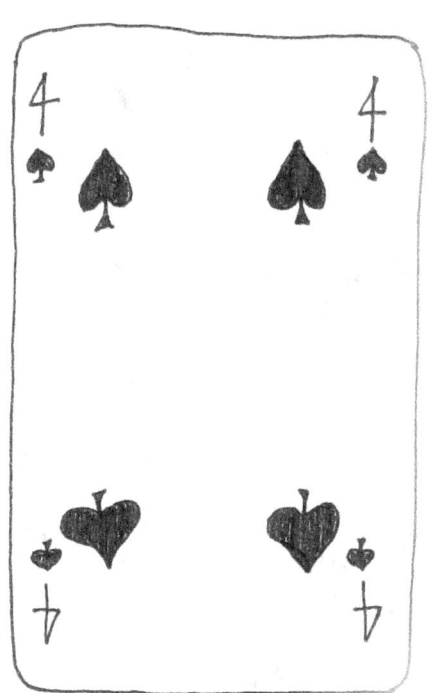

OK, LET'S PLAY A GAME:

IF IT'S HIGER THAN 7, YOU MOVE TO PORTLAND, ME
IF IT'S LOWER THAN 7, YOU MOVE TO PORTLAND, OR

AND I DRAW A 7.... DAMN.

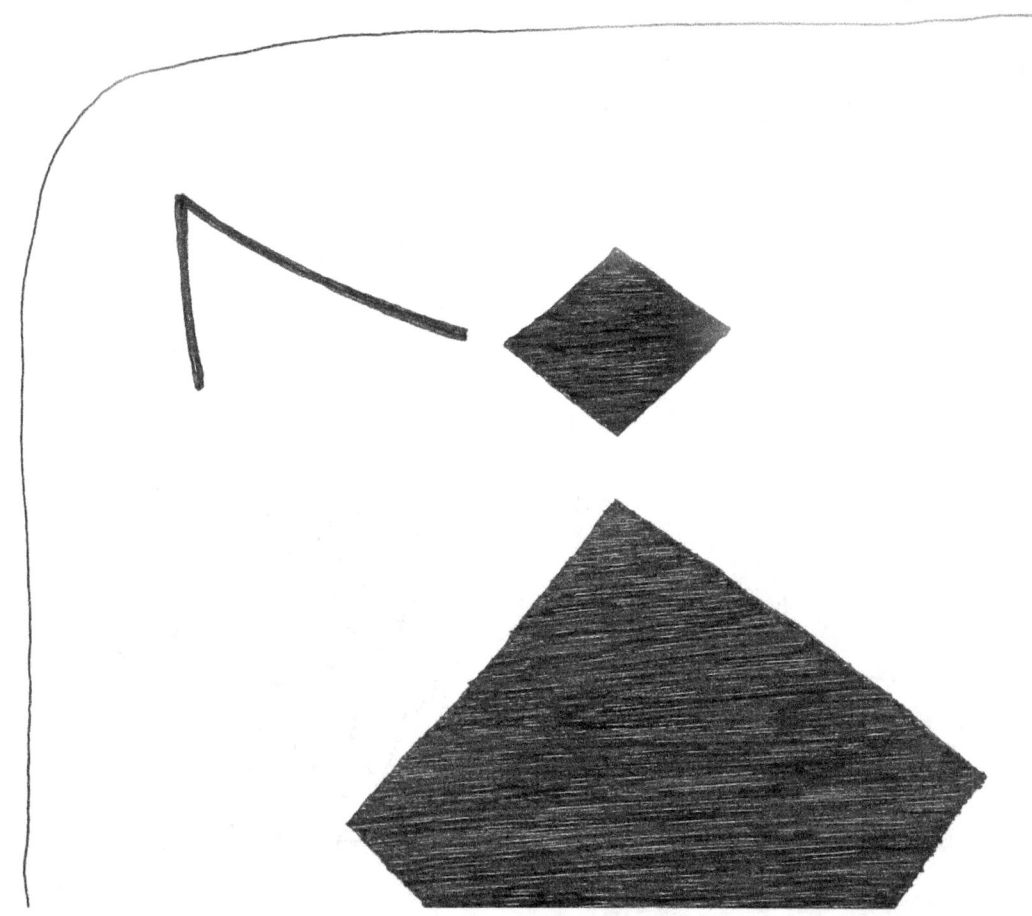
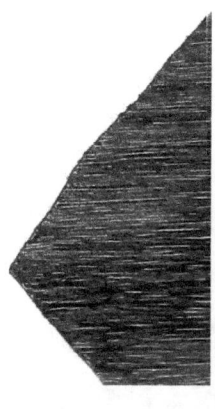

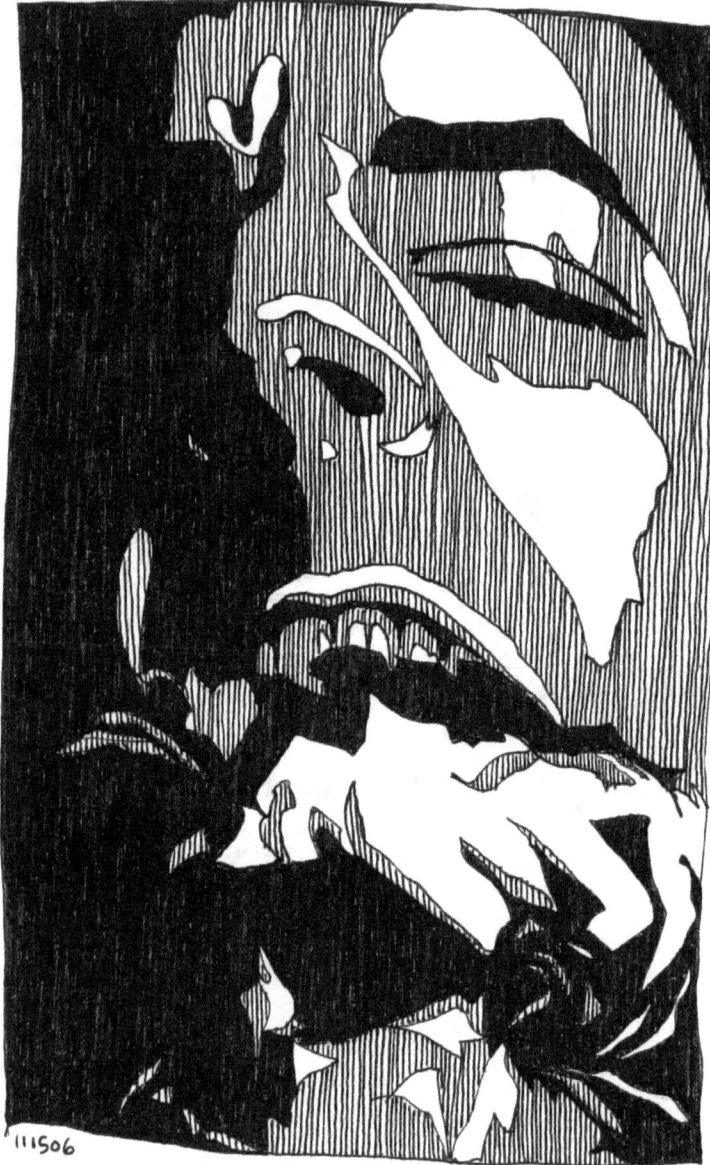

111506

TO

111606

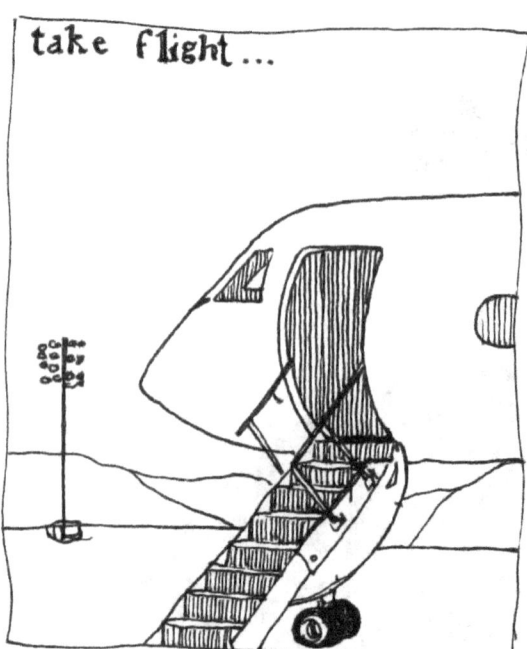

take flight...

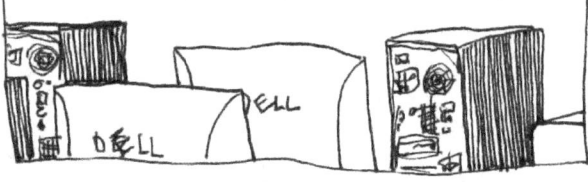

TODAY, CLASS, WE ARE GOING TO TALK ABOUT HOW MUCH I SUCK AT GRAPHIC DESIGN!

DELL

DELL

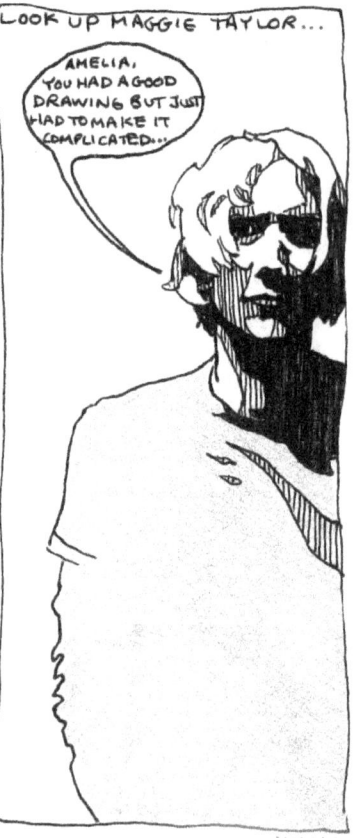

LOOK UP MAGGIE TAYLOR...

AMELIA, YOU HAD A GOOD DRAWING BUT JUST HAD TO MAKE IT COMPLICATED...

YOU WROTE TO ME AGAIN - I WAS COMPLETELY SURPRISED. I'D THINK ABOUT YOU EVERY ONCE IN A WHILE. BUT IT'S BEEN SO LONG SINCE I'D HEARD FROM YOU. NOW, I WANT TO TALK TO YOU AGAIN - SEE YOU AGAIN. BUT ONLY IN THE HEALTHIEST OF WAYS. I WAS REMEMBERING WHAT YOUR FACE LOOKS LIKE AND YOUR SMILE, TOO. THOSE FEW DAYS WE LOCKED OURSELVES IN YOUR ROOM AND JUST TALKED AND LOVED EACH OTHER'S COMPANY - AND THOSE WALKS - I CHERISHED OUR TALKS - MAYBE OUR PATHS WILL MERGE AGAIN - MAYBE NOT. BUT I'M SO GLAD TO JUST WRITE TO YOU AGAIN - ■

11·18·06

111606

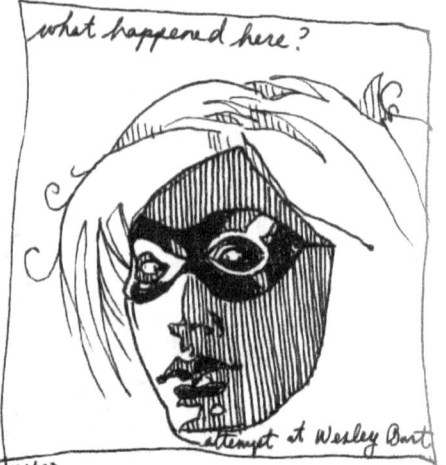

what happened here?

attempt at Wesley Burt

111606

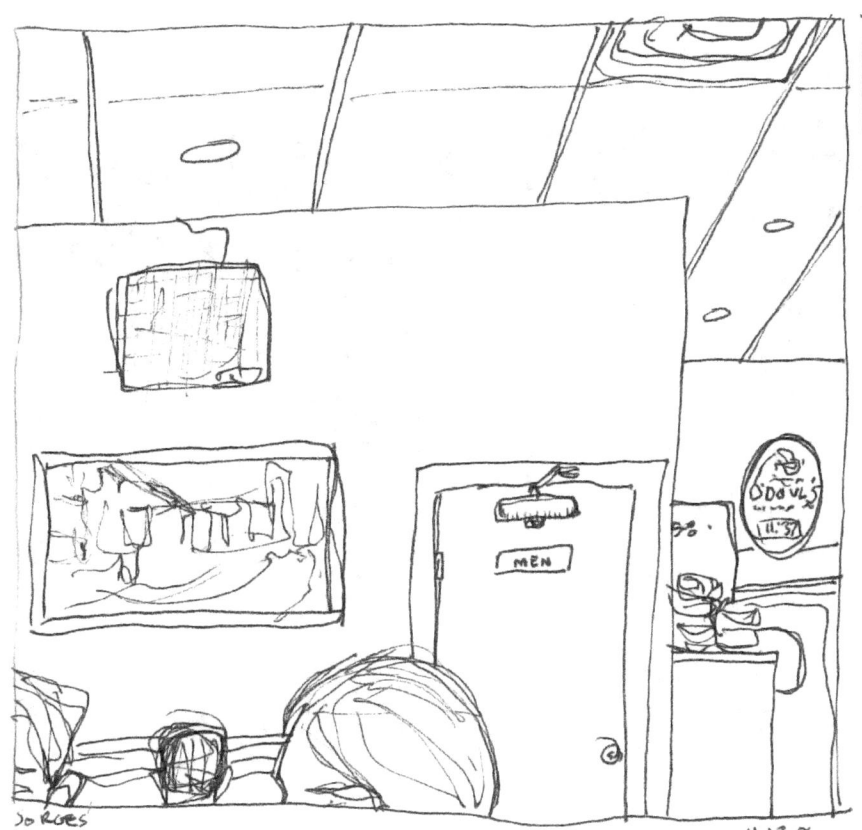
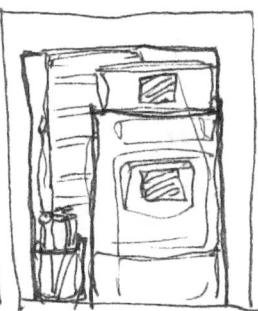
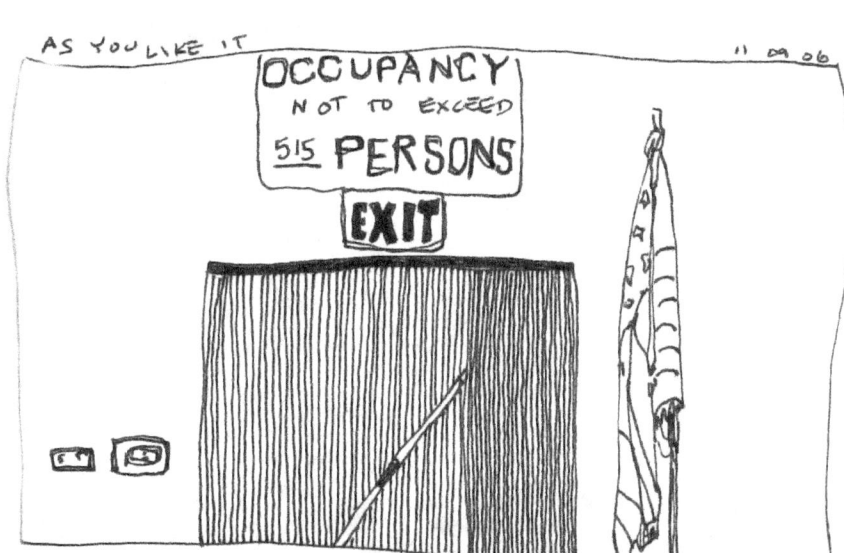
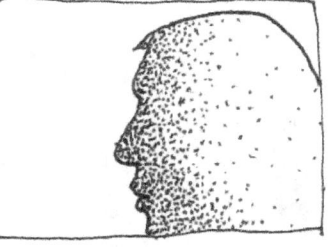
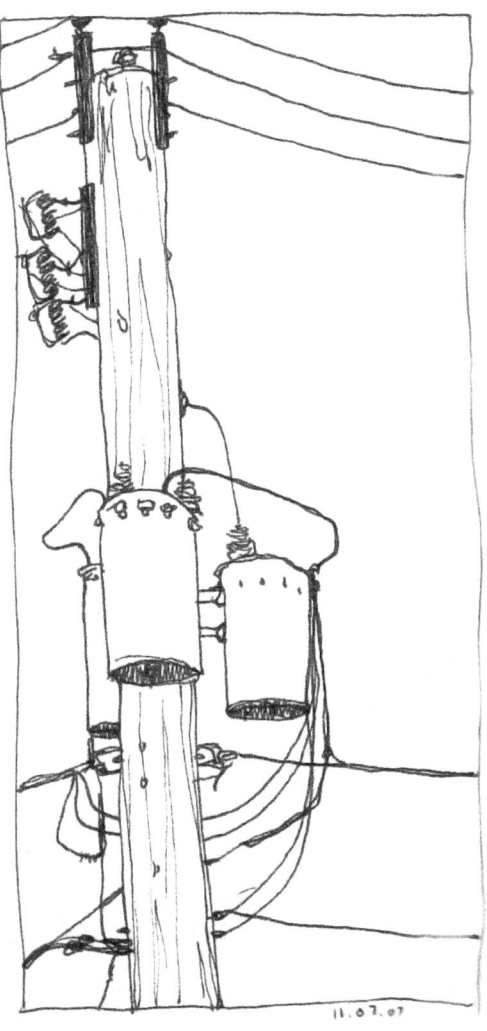

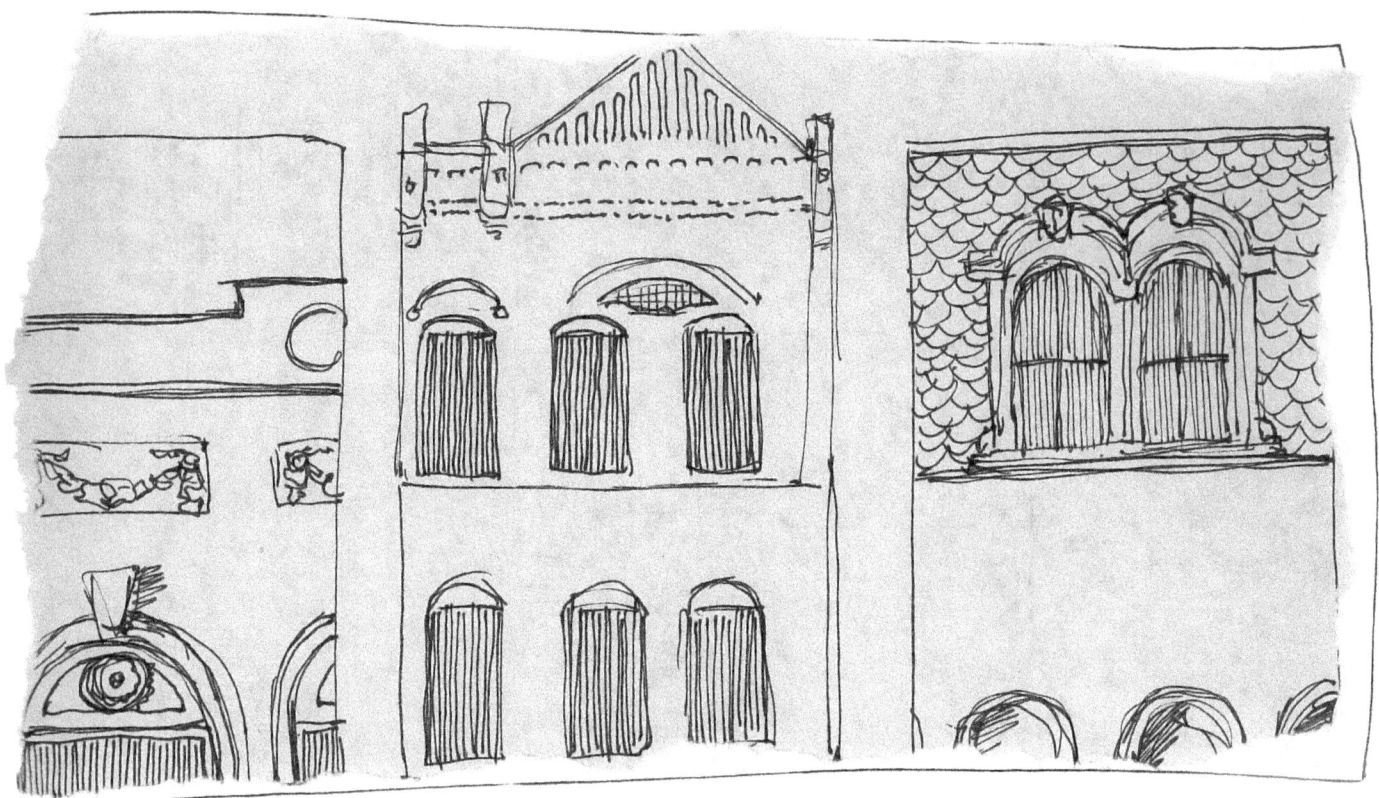

YOU'RE ASKING ME TO KNOWINGLY
FACE MY DEATH.

STRANGER THAN FICTION

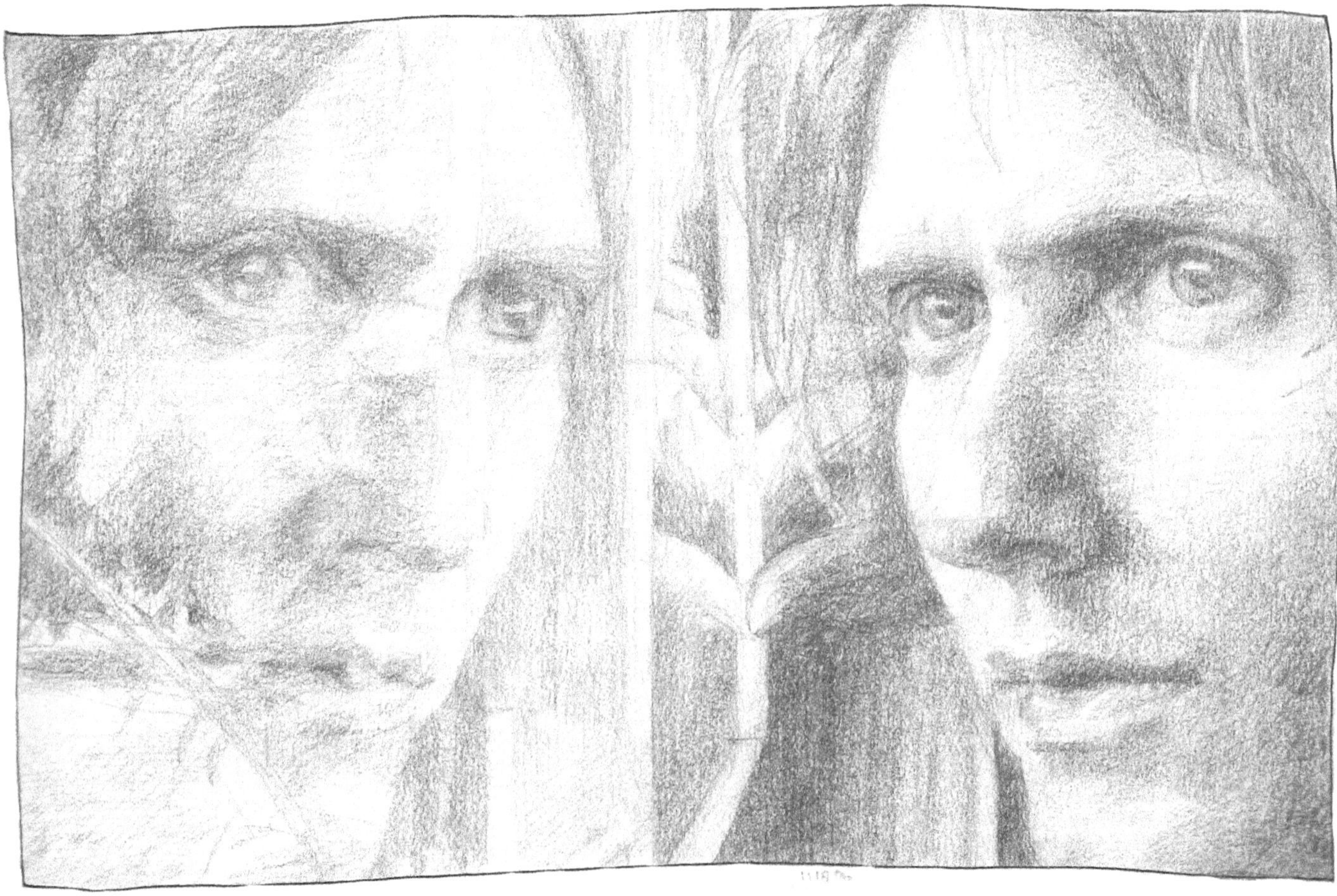

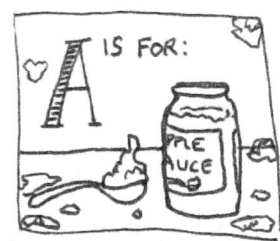
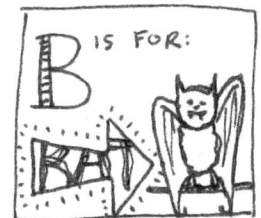
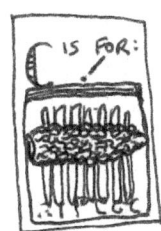
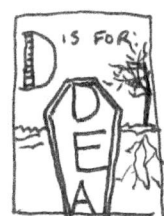
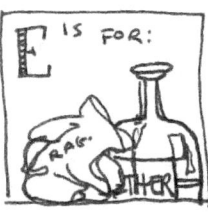
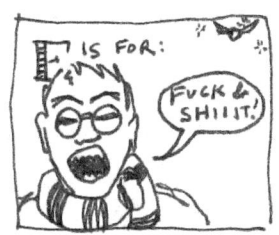
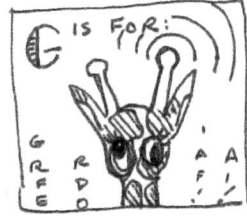
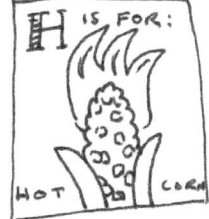
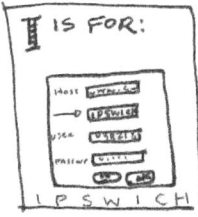
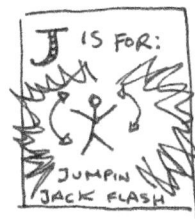
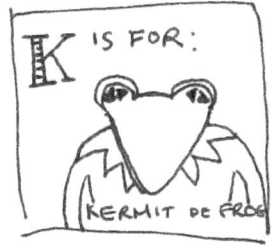
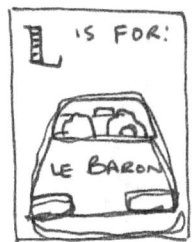
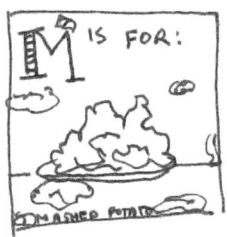
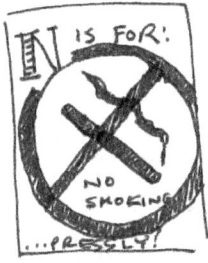
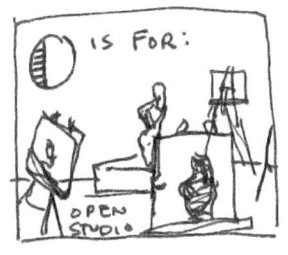
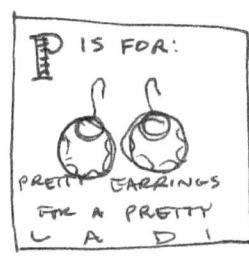
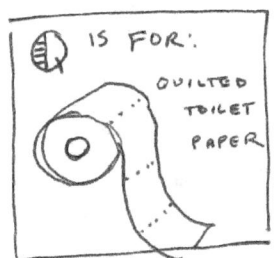
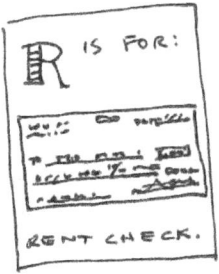
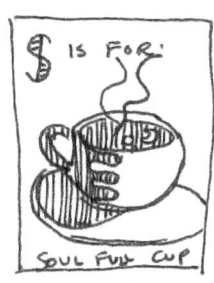
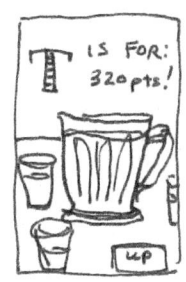
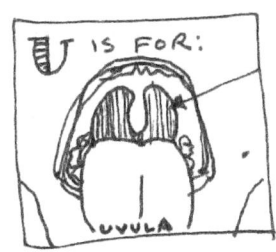
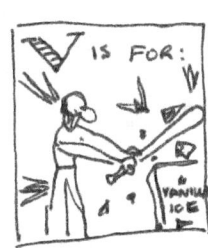
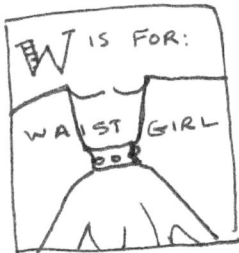
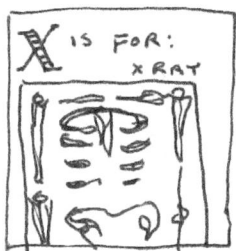
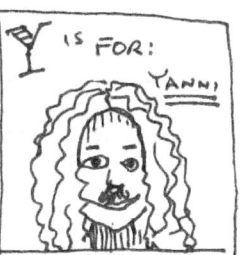
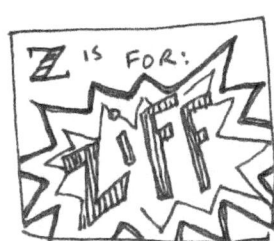

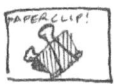
PAPERCLIP!

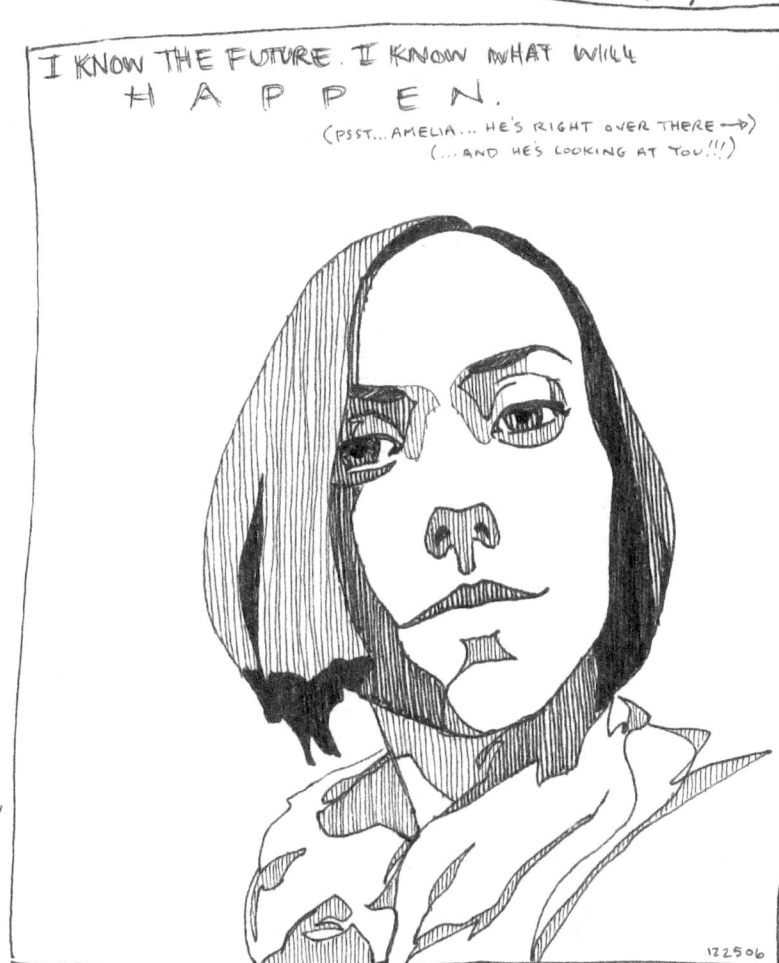

I couldn't sleep either. the radiator in the bathroom woke me up. but once awake I just lay there thinking too much. possibilities churning all over the place. so I got up and wrote and wrote everything down and even then, when I got back in bed, I kept on...

I KNOW THE FUTURE. I KNOW WHAT WILL H A P P E N.

(PSST... AMELIA... HE'S RIGHT OVER THERE →)
(...AND HE'S LOOKING AT YOU!!!)

122506

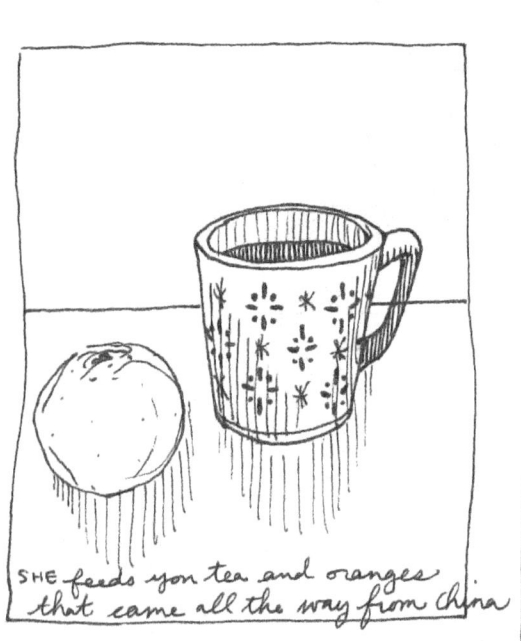

SHE feeds you tea and oranges
that came all the way from China

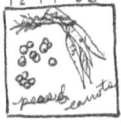
12·17·06·
peanuts, carnitas

let's send notes back and forth in bottles. let's go swimming in the pacific ocean without our clothes. let's have rain drop races. let's act out plays switching between actors and characters rapidly. let's laugh so hard we can't stop and tears begin trickling down our cheeks and we have trouble breathing. let's invent our own constellations. let's play scrabble with only our invented words and accompanying definitions. let's just lay next to each other with our faces just inches apart and talk about all that we know and in that find more to know. let's ride trains. let's plant a garden. let's learn how to tango and then tango in the kitchen naked. let's weave our hair together and spend a day as siamese twins. let's kiss all the time and more. let's sing in empty echo-y stairwells. let's giggle and have marshmellow fights. let's love each other everyday as if it were the first&last days we have together. let's soak up every last bit of beauty that comes our way. let's find ourselves in each other, and stand amazed and in awe. let's do this - all of it, together.

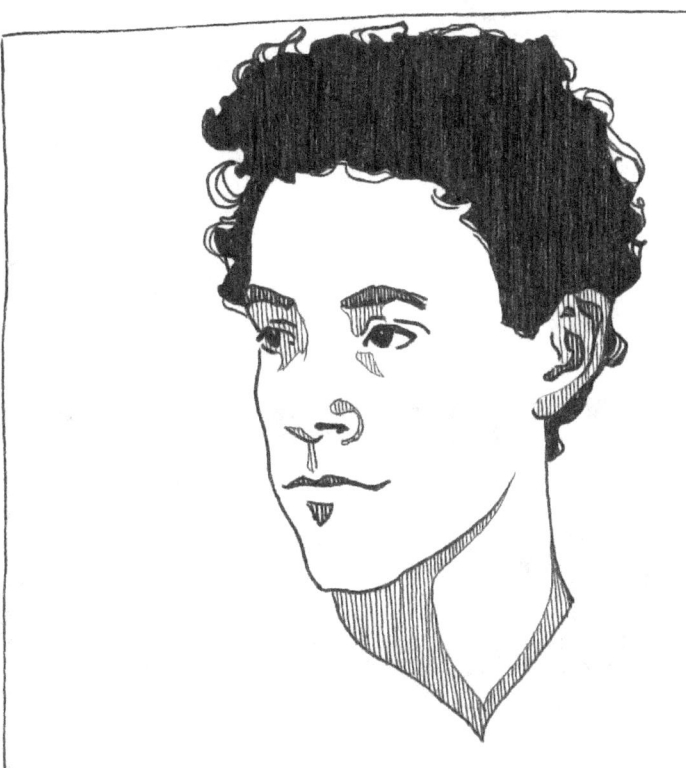

It's so great to meet someone who knows how to play.

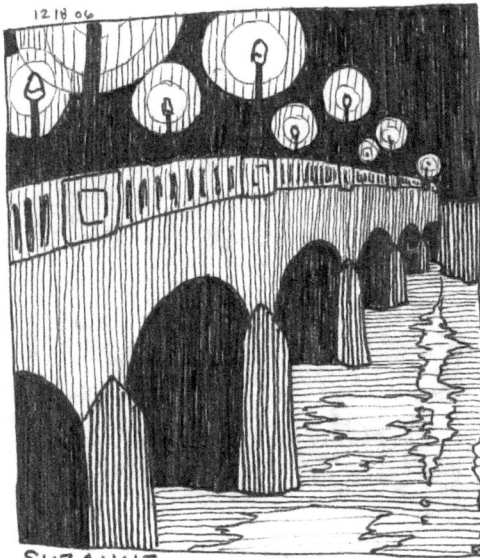

1218 06

SUZANNE TAKES YOU DOWN TO
HER PLACE BY THE RIVER

"THE WORLD GETS UP WITH YOU, AND BEGINNING GLISTENS ON THE BREAKING-PLACE OF OUR FAILURE" AND LORD KNOWS I'VE HAD A ROUGH COUPLE OF YEARS, TOO. I FEEL SO MUCH BETTER TODAY - WHAT HAVE I BEEN MISSING?

WAITING FOR THE TRAIN.

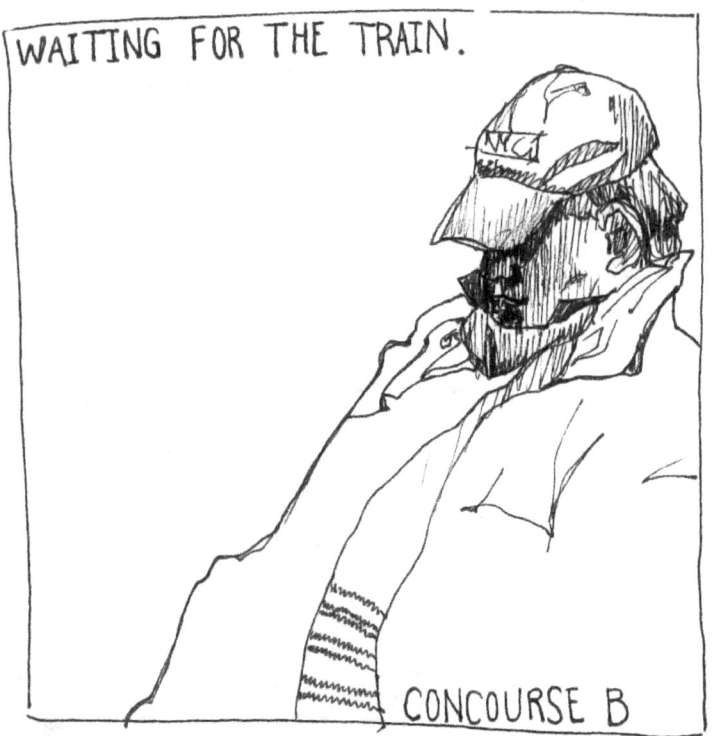

CONCOURSE B

I'm on the train from Buffalo to Chicago. I decided to get a sleeper car, and it was well worth the extra cost. The train was late last night by on hour and a half and we're still running slightly behind. I had a good night's sleep and the continental breakfast. I liked the waiter - I wonder how long he's been a waiter on trains... I hate to be stereotypical but he's an older black guy. I sort of want to brush my teeth. I love hearing the train whistle just up ahead. My little table that I am using has a checker/chess board on it... but I am all alone with no one to play with. Now I am in Chicago now - after hitchi aasy se sleeping my heavy shit, I'm now parked under a very loud TV talking about old cheerleaders. Jesus. A Jazzy? A fucking old person chair called a "Jazzy"?!! Ohhh Amtrak is paging Joan Parker. I need to find my baby daddy, my lady daddy... paternity. t eats in the north concourse B lounge. There is this woman on the train with a terrible st utter and the attendant is talking about the 90 mph wind that held up a train for nine hours. The sky is swarming with seagulls - we just pulled in to Milwakee, WI. next stop, Pewakee ...oh joy oh je

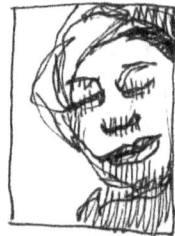

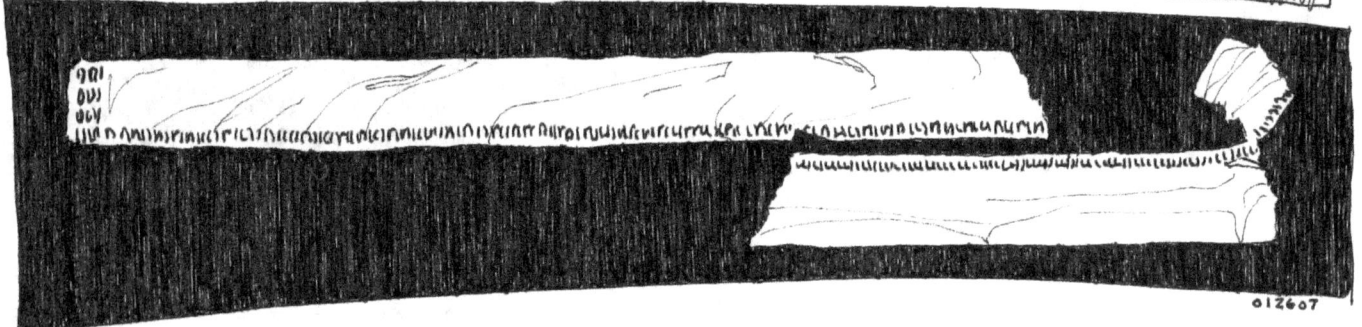

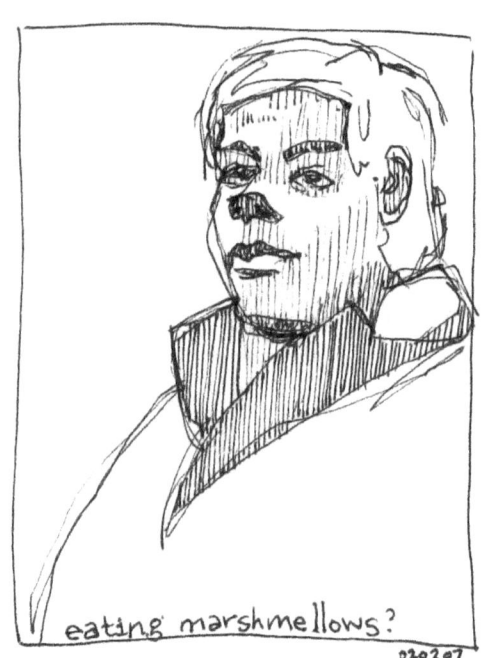

eating marshmellows?

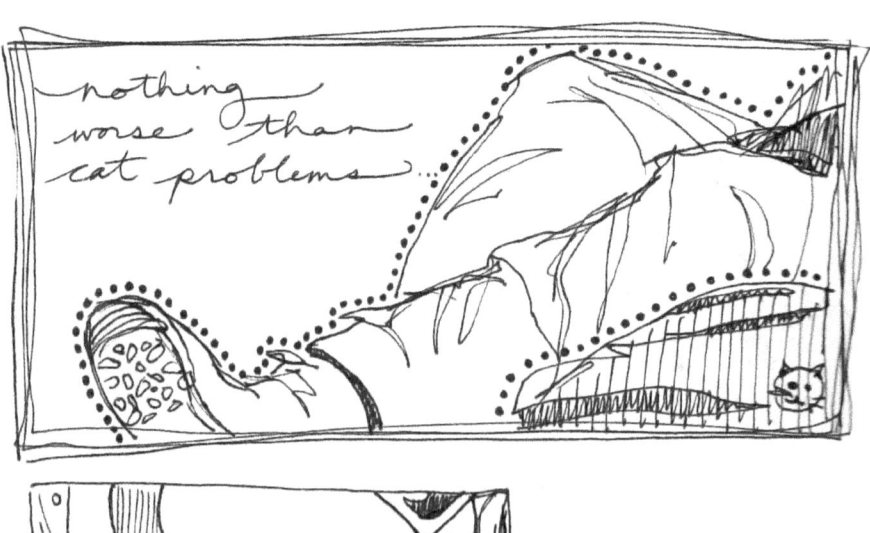

nothing worse than cat problems...

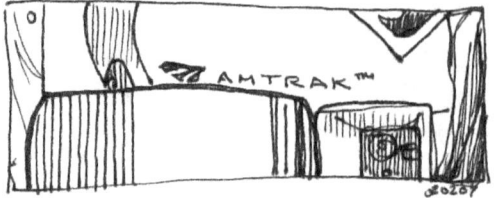

AMTRAK™

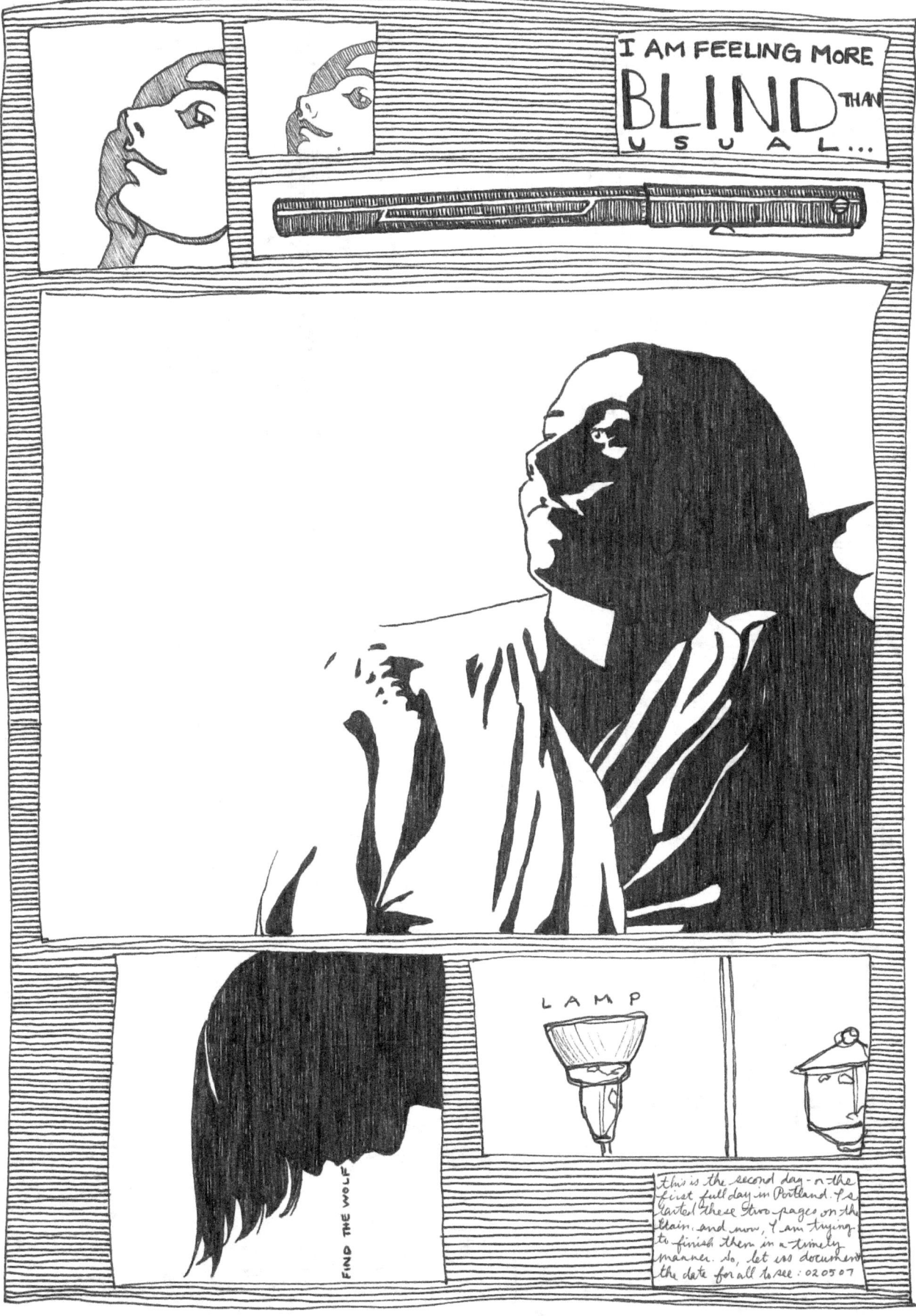

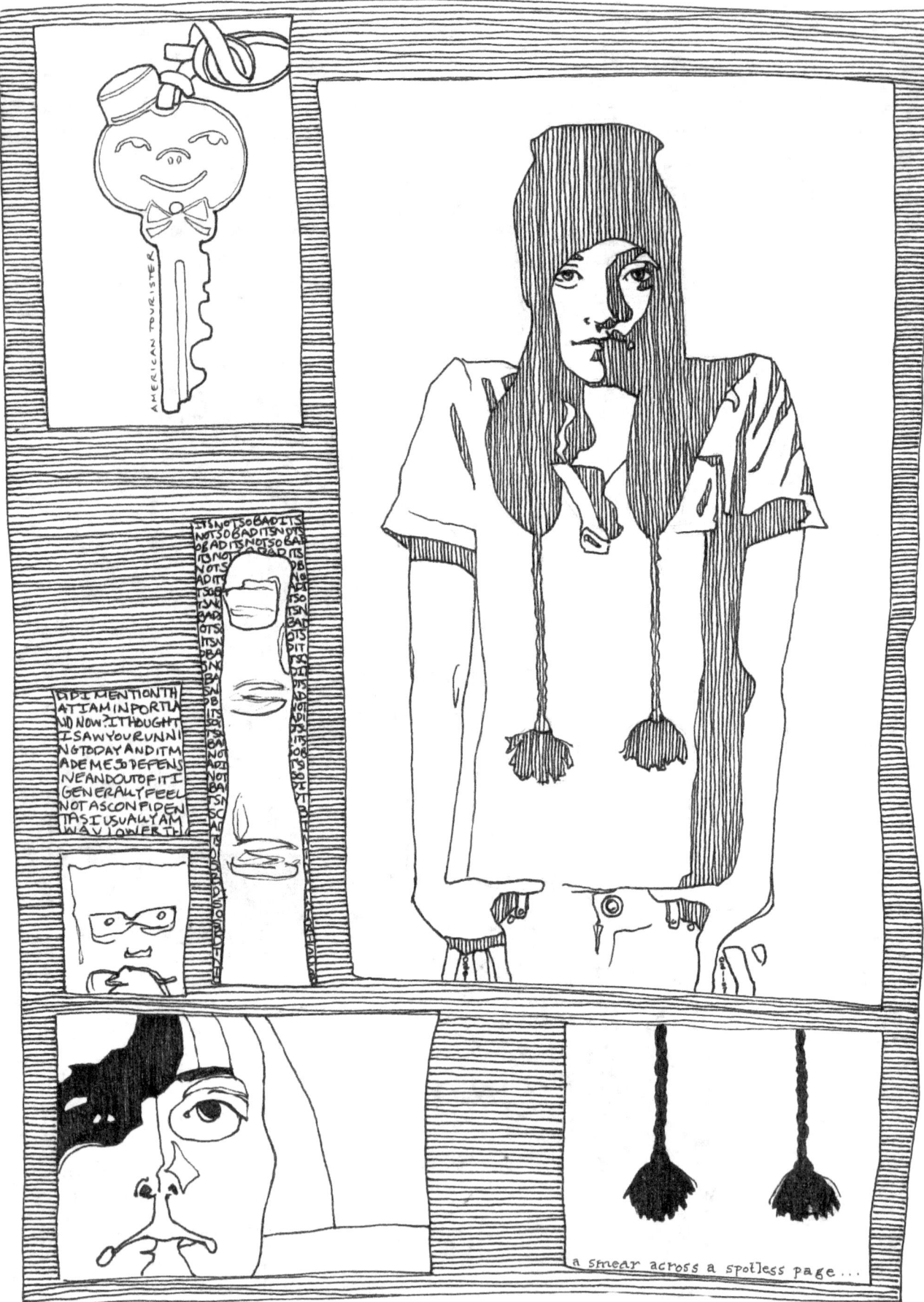

AMERICAN TOURISTER

ITSNOTSOBADITS
NOTSOBADITSNOTS
OBADITSNOTSOBA
DITSNOTSOBADITS
NOTSO

DIDIMENTIONTH
ATIAMINPORTLA
NDNOW?ITHOUGHT
ISAWYOURUNNI
NGTODAYANDITM
ADEMESODEFENS
IVEANDOUTOFITI
GENERALLYFEEL
NOTASCONFIDEN
TASIUSUALLYAM
WAYLOWERTH

a smear across a spotless page...

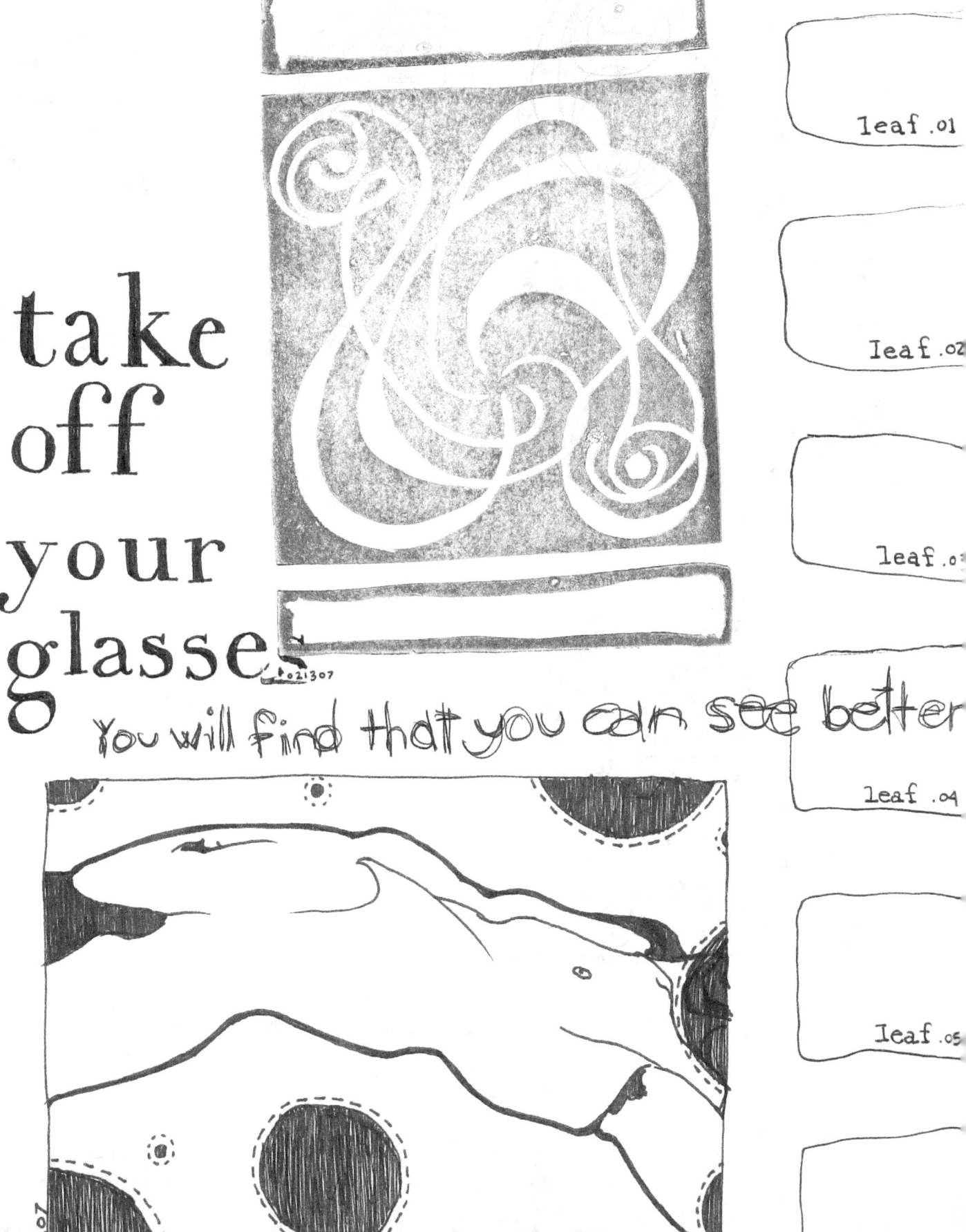

take
off
your
glasses

you will find that you can see better

leaf .01

leaf .02

leaf .0

leaf .04

leaf .05

leaf .06

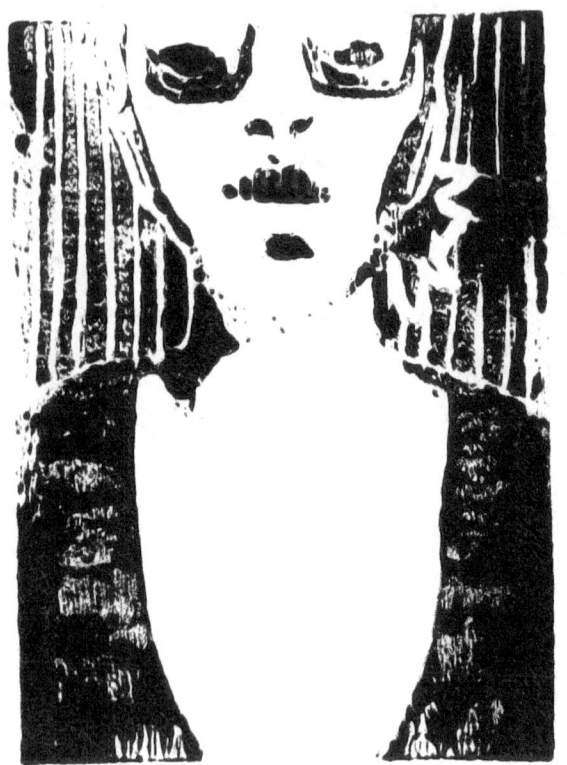

NOV. 11 1972

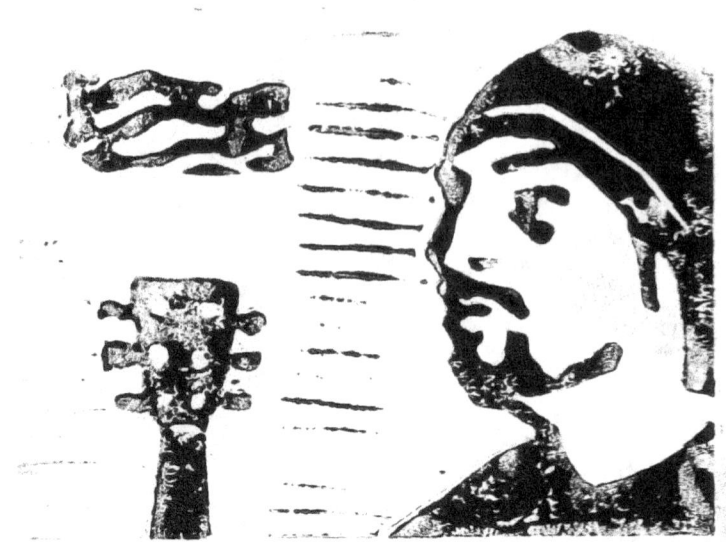

MAY 01 1972

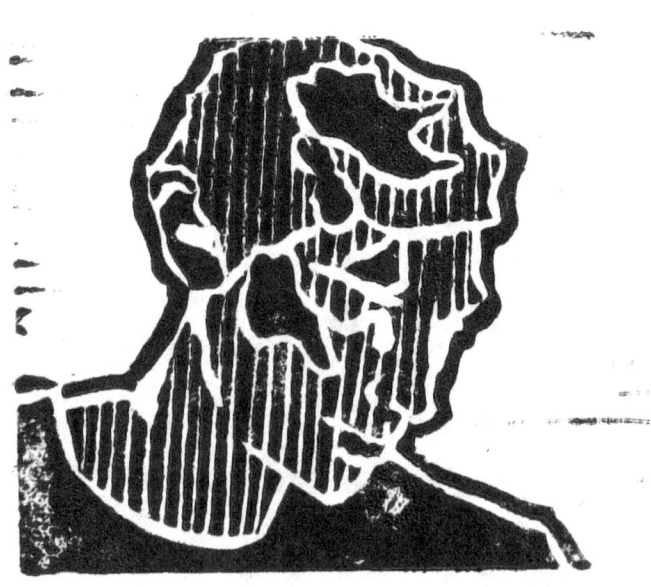

JUL. 27 1972

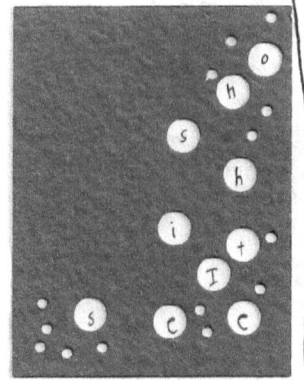

A HOMELESS MAN GAVE
ME THE KEY TO HIS HEART
ON THE ESPLANADE. 08.29.07

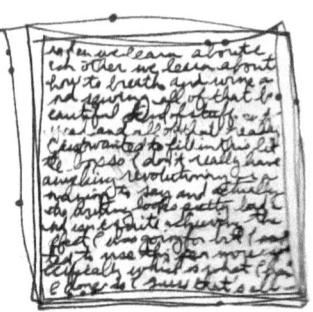

Amelia Hernas — bio & statement
It seems like every six to nine
months I decide to drastically
change my plans. Each time,
I wipe the dust from my cheeks
and think to myself, "well, that
should be the last time I do that
for a good long while." now, I
realize that changing directions
is not the same as being direction-
less — especially when on that
epic road trip called making art.

091207

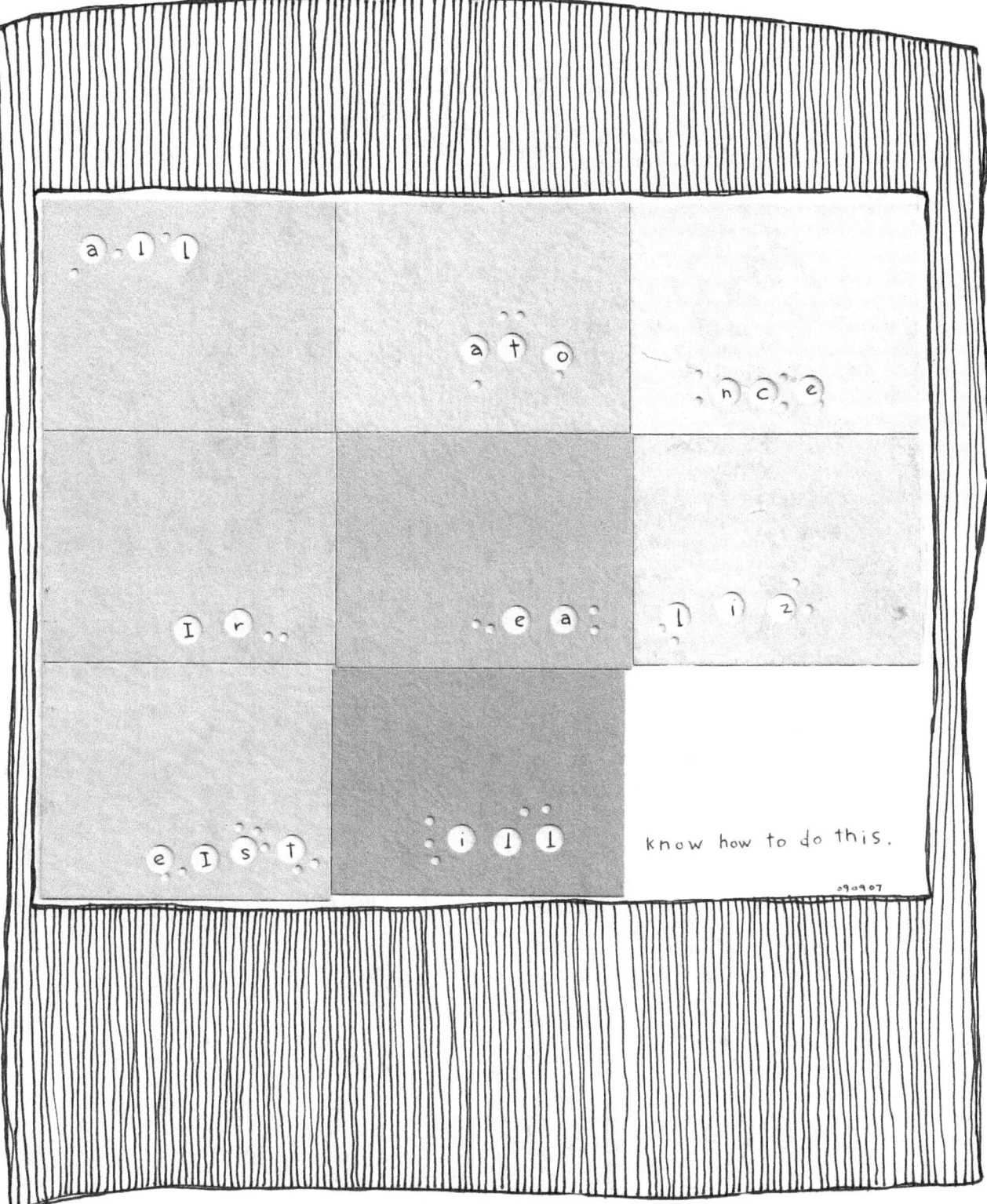

know how to do this.

GIVE UP HOPE.

maybe I just might, Mr. Orwell.

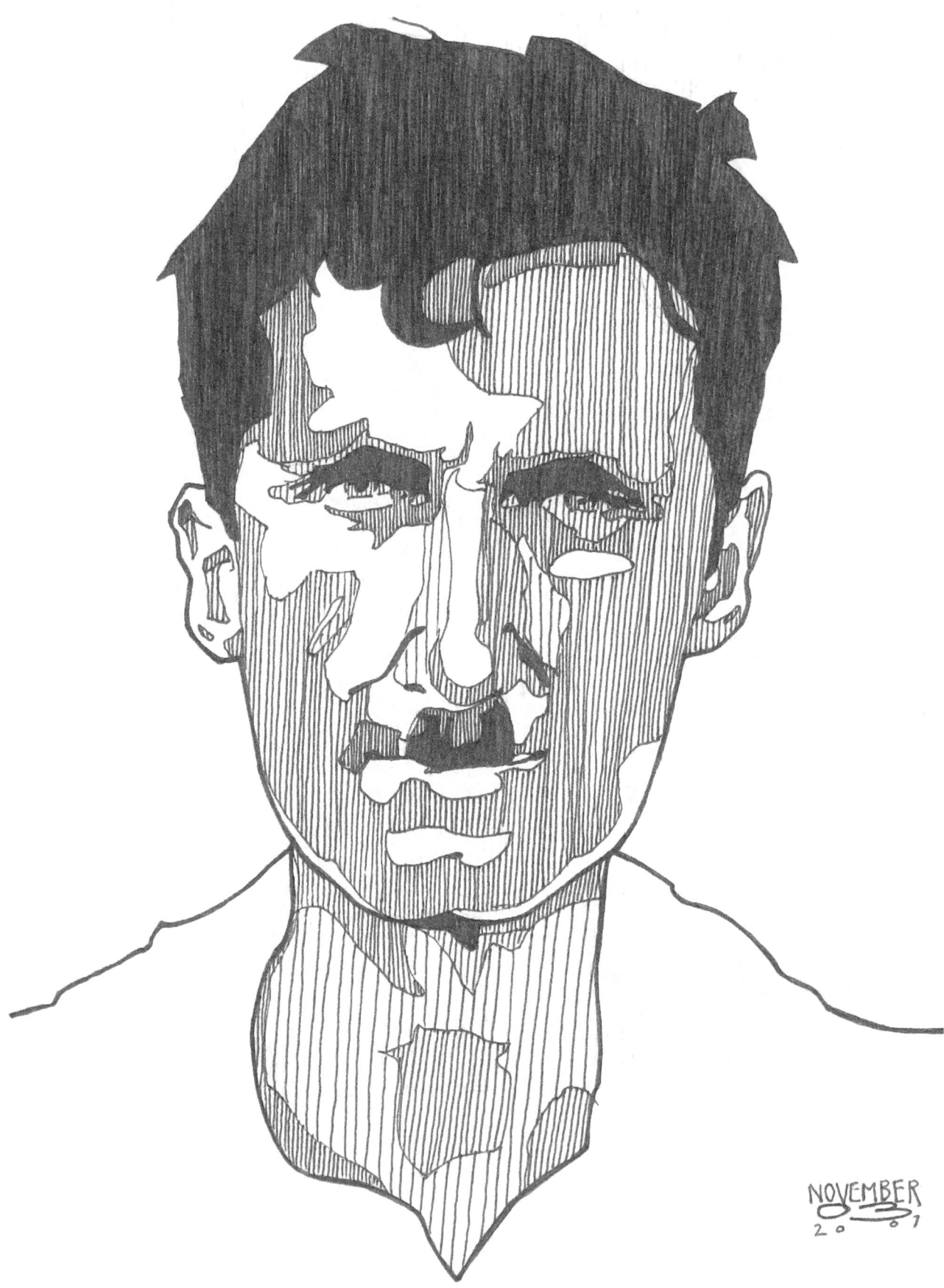

NOVEMBER
20 03

MY ONE-PAGE BIOGRAPHY FOR GEORGE WHITMAN.

SOMETIMES, IN THOSE STILL MOMENTS WHEN ALL THE REST BUSTLES BUSILY, PURRING ON ALL SIDES, MAKING MY BONES MORE STURDY — SOMETIMES I WONDER IN HOW MANY PHOTOGRAPHS I APPEAR. PHOTOS TAKEN BY MY PARENTS, MY FAMILY, FOR SCHOOL YEARBOOKS, BY FRIENDS, ARTISTS, FOR PASSPORTS, DRIVERS LICENSES, BY LOVERS, AND TOURISTS, MYSELF. JUST LAST NIGHT, STANDING AT THE WINDOW IN THE LIBRARY, ONE OF THE TOURISTS OUTSIDE THE SHOP CAUGHT SIGHT OF ME LOOKING OUT AT NOTRE DAME BEING RIPPLED WITH ORANGE AND WHITE LIGHT BY A BOAT TOUR THAT WAS PASSING BY. SHE ANGLED UP HER CAMERA AND NOW THERE EXISTS ANOTHER PHOTO OF ME. ① HOW MANY ARE THERE? THOUSANDS? HUNDREDS OF THOUSANDS? MORE? AND IF THERE WAS SOME WAY TO GATHER THEM ALL UP- ALL AT ONCE — AND ARRANGE THEM IN CHRONOLOGICAL ORDER, WOULD THE WHOLE MASS OF THEM EXPLAIN MY LIFE TO A STRANGER WITHOUT THE NEED FOR THE PROPER TRANSLATION FROM MY LANGUAGE TO ANOTHER'S? ✗ JUST WORDS FORMED BY MY LIPS, FROZEN IN PLANNED AND UNPLANNED LINES AND CURVES JUST SENTENCES BUILT BY MY EYEBROWS AND SPIDERY FINGERS AND WILD HAIR ✗ THEN I WENT TO SEE LA JACONDE TODAY. I STOOD TO HER RIGHT, FACING THE SAME THRONG OF TINY, SILVER, FLASHING CAMERAS. HUNDREDS OF PICTURES MUST HAVE BEEN TAKEN IN JUST THOSE FIFTEEN MINUTES I SPENT WATCHING PEOPLE FALLING OVER EACH FOR A BETTER VIEW, I REALIZED IN THAT HOT, NOISY ROOM HOW ALL MY LIFE, I'VE EITHER WANTED TO BE THE WOMAN IN THE PAINTING OR THE WOMAN WHO PAINTED IT. NO — I WANT TO BE BOTH. ① THIS IS NOT SO MUCH DIFFERENT A DESIRE THAN A WRITER WANTING TO BE READ OR A MUSICIAN WANTING TO BE HEARD —— AND MOREOVER, BY THOUSANDS OF PEOPLE GENERATIONS TO COME? AMBITIOUS? I AM AMBITIOUS. ② WHEN I WAS FOUR, MY PARENTS AND I WERE STROLLING DOWN TO A SMALL LOCAL MARKET TO GET ICECREAM OR SOMEOTHER SUGARY LADEN DELIGHT. A MAN WITH A POLAROID INSTANT CAMERA WALKED UP TO MY MOTHER & FATHER AND ASKED THEM IF HE COULD TAKE A PHOTO OF US. THEY AGREED, AND WE ALL POSED AND SMILED. AFTER THE CAMERA FLASHED AND WHIRRED, HE HANDED THEM THE GRAY, GLOSSY PRINT, THANKED THEM & THEN WENT HIS WAY. MY FATHER BLEW GENTLY ON THE PHOTO AS THE GHOSTLY IMAGE BECAME MORE CLEAR. AND THERE I WAS IN THE CENTER OF THE PHOTO SHYLY SMILING — ONLY MY PARENTS' FEET, ANKLES & CALVES COULD BE SEEN. THE STRANGER ONLY REALLY WANTED TO TAKE A PICTURE OF ME. ③ I HAVE BEEN KNOWN TO ASK STRANGERS FOR THEIR PHOTOS, TOO. FACES FASCINATE ME. I'VE SPENT HUNDREDS OF HOURS BY NOW, DRAWING AND PAINTING FACES. IT IS TRUE THAT SELF PORTRAITS SEEM TO TAKE PRIORITY SOME DAYS, BUT THAT IS ONLY WHEN I'M BEING TO SHY OR INTROSPECTIVE TO ASK OTHERS FOR THEIR PHOTOS

I FINISHED THE REST ON THE COMPUTER...

                                              ... AND NEVER LET JEFF READ IT.

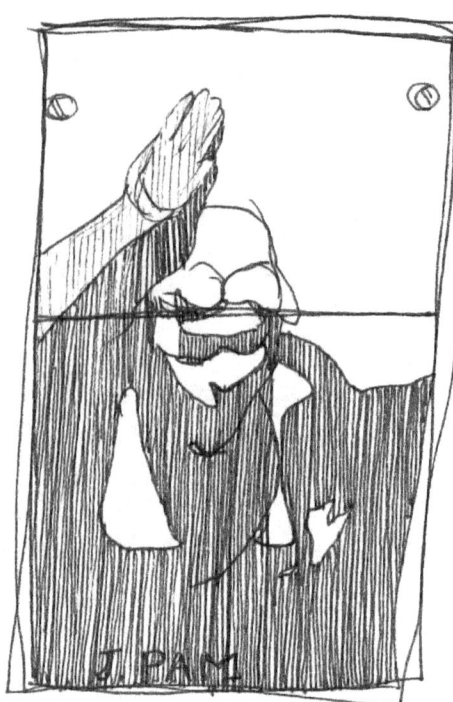

J. PAM!

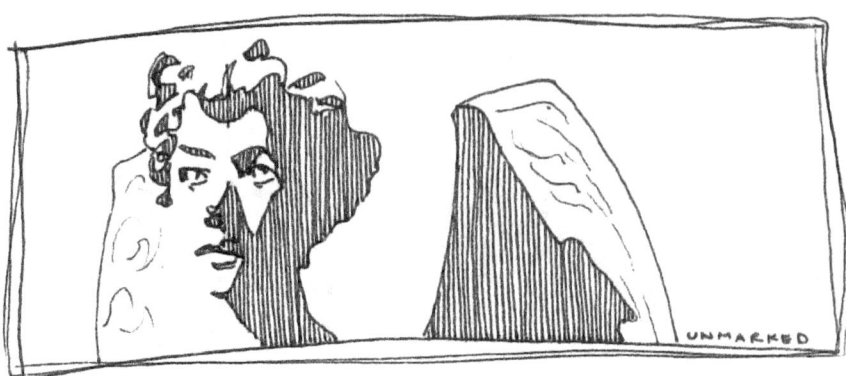

UNMARKED

SPLEEN

J'AI TANT AIMÉ L'AMOUR
LES FLEURS ET LES NUAGES!

JE N'AI PLUS DE COURAGE
POUR LUTTER CHAQUE JOUR.
MON CŒUR PÈSE TROP LOURD
LA VIE EST MONOTONE
ET LA CHANSON RÉSONNE
DE MON DERNIER AMOUR,
PARFOIS, COMME UN GLAS SOURD...
AINSI VA-T-IL DES RÊVES
UN RIEN NOUS LES ENLÈVE,
LE TEMPS D'AIMER EST COURT!
DÉJÀ VOICI LE TOUR
DE LA BLÊME DÉTRESSE
QUI SUCCÈDE À L'IVRESSE
ET APPELLE AU SECOURS.

J'AVAIS SOIF DE TENDRESSE
POUR BERCER MON AMOUR...

FAMILLE JAVAL

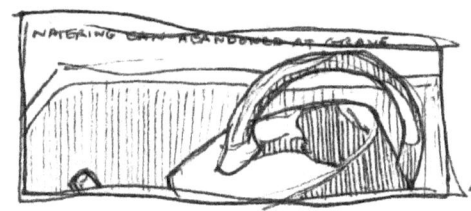

WATERING CAN ABANDONED AT GRAVE

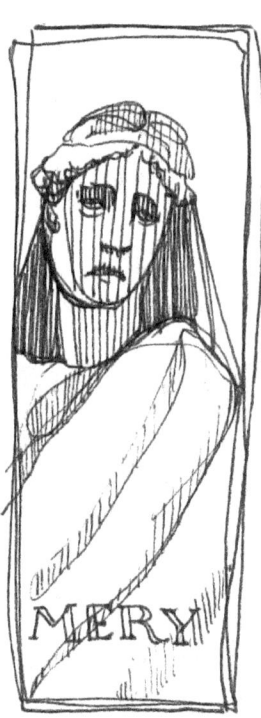

MERY

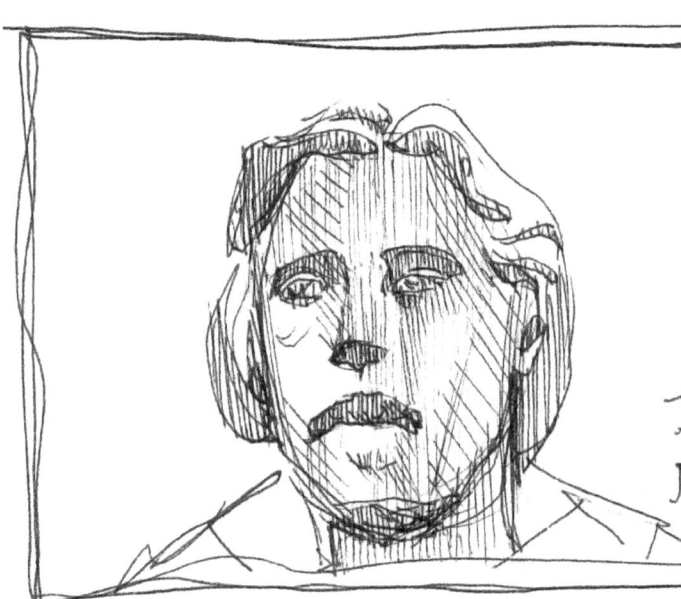

a terrible drawing
of ("my hands were cold...")

JEAN BERNARD LÉON
FOUCAULT

CIMET-
IÈRE · M
ONTMAR-
TRE · 12.11.07

M	T	W	T	F	S	S
12 CIMETIÈRE MONTMARTRE FLORIAN	**13** ERRANDS FOODS, GOODS ONE LAST DAY MAKING MOONMAKERS	**14** WALK! CENTRE POMPIDOU TOTONY'S @ 11ish IMPROV @ 8:30 4E	**15** MUSÉE D'ORSAY & CHAMPS ELYSÉES?	**16** BASES? POLITICS? PLAGE? LOUVRE @ 6-10	**17** CRISE! @ 6:54	**18** TO KÖLN @ 6:55 KÖLN ADO FRANKFURT TO GERMANY KASSEL AGE
19 KASSEL SHOPPING TRIP ANTONIO'S	**20** VIADUCT FIELD TRIP, GROCERIES AGE	**21** MEET @ RATHAUS 5:20 PM TRANSIT TO GERMANY	**22** PARTI THANKS-GIVING WITH AGE!	**23** RITE OF SPRING TOUR KASSEL EXPLORE DAY	**24** THANKSGIVING W/ MORE TIME/EFFORT CINNAMON BUNS, PARTY W/ AGE	**25** OBATZERIE SLIDES, POKER? BACH AGE
26 KASSEL CHRISTMAS MARKET OPENS!	**27**	**28** MORE XMAS MRKT & LESSON @ 7:15	**29** LAUNDRY	**30** ECONOMICS W/ AGE POSTPONED?	**1** NOLLENDORFEL FIRE	**2** FLICKR EMAIL TXT ANTONIO
3 VERY. GET REFUND TRANSIT TO PARIS, LEAVE @ 10:39 ARRIVE @ 16:34 PARTY AMANDA	**4** DROP OFF PORTRAIT DAY WITH JEFF. RODIN MUSÉE (MOREAU MUSÉE) ANTONIO'S	**5** LEAVE PARIS @ 1:00 ARRIVE IN PHILLY @ 5PM XMAS PARTY	**6** SLEEP HAIRCUT ANNA	**7** BUS TO B'MORE AROUND NOON?	**8** HOLIDAY DINNER IN B'MORE ADAM & SARAH	**9** BUS TO NYC @ 2ish
10 CONEY ISLAND $0 END!	**11** ART MUSEUM / BRAU / DRAW / WALK ALEX	**12**	**13** CYRANO DE BERGERAC @ 8?	**14** BUS TO BINGHAMTON AFTERNOON/EVENING PARTY!	**15** REHEARSE W/ CHAD 1-5PM TOM S @ 5PM	**16** HORSE GARAGE REHEARSE WITH MORE
17 MAIL ✓ GIFTS TO PDX LOGISTICAL ERRANDS DENNY'S W/ PRESSLY @ 9PM	**18** MEET WITH DAVE — MEET WITH GINNIE THEN LUNCH W/ SHARLA	**19** REHEARSE W/ CHAD FAMILY DAY @ SALVO! TEETH @ 11am	**20** REHEARSE W/ MIKE 2:30?? 5:30-7:30	**21** PLAY @ 7:00 @ OUL FULL CUP	**22** PICK UP AGE & HOLGER @ JFK [I AM @ HOME THO.]	**23** TRIM TREE, PLUG N' TOSS ALL THAT GOOD STUFF

N
O
V

D
E
C

MASTER PLAN

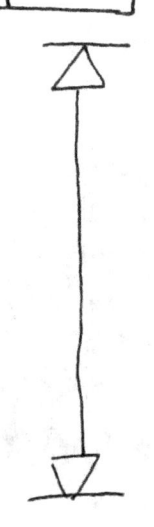

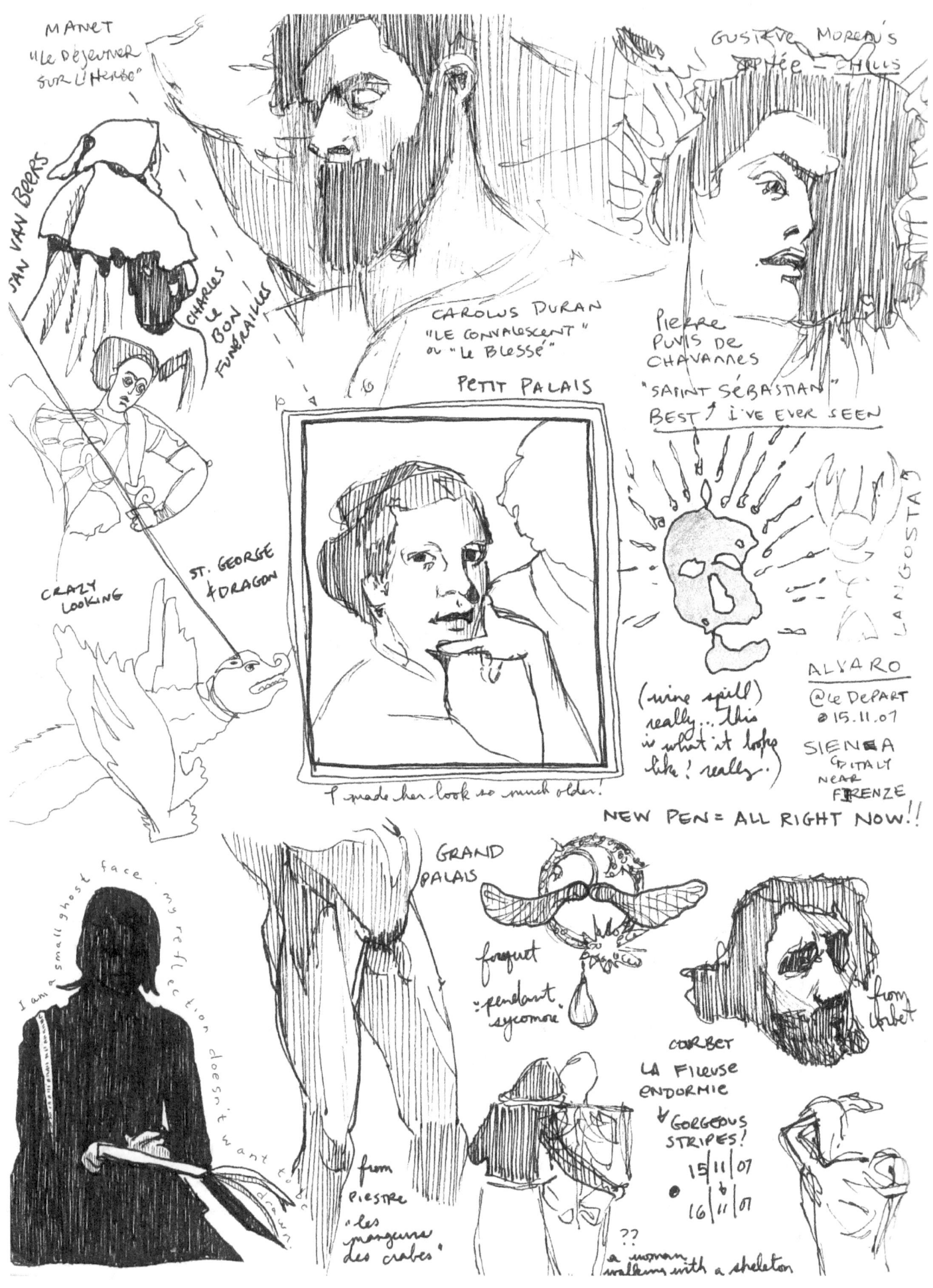

MANET
"LE DÉJEUNER
SUR L'HERBE"

JAN VAN BEERS

CHARLES LE BON FUNÉRAILLES

CAROLUS DURAN
"LE CONVALESCENT"
OU "LE BLESSÉ"

PETIT PALAIS

GUSTAVE MOREAU'S
ORPHÉE — CHILLS

PIERRE PUVIS DE CHAVANNES
"SAINT SÉBASTIAN"
BEST I'VE EVER SEEN

CRAZY LOOKING

ST. GEORGE & DRAGON

I made her look so much older!

(wine spill) really... this is what it looks like! really.)

LANGOSTA?

ALVARO
@ LE DEPART
@ 15.11.07

SIENA
ITALY
NEAR
FIRENZE

NEW PEN = ALL RIGHT NOW!!

I am a small ghost face... my reflection doesn't want to be drawn

GRAND PALAIS

from PIESTRE
"les mangeurs des crabes"

forget
"pendant sycomore"

CORBET
LA FILEUSE
ENDORMIE
& GORGEOUS
STRIPES!
15/11/07
to
16/11/07

from Corbet

??
a woman walking with a skeleton

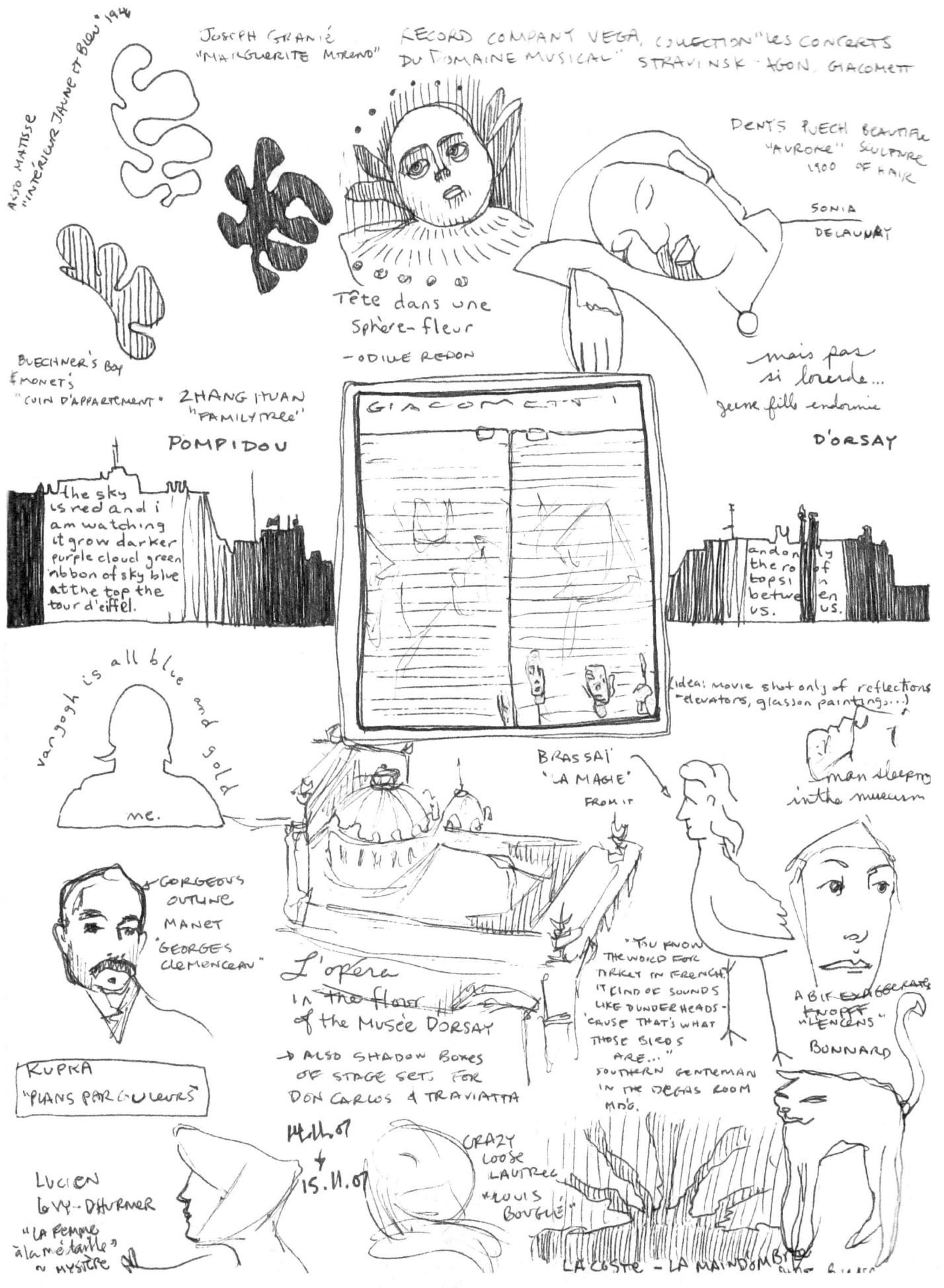

ALSO MATISSE "INTÉRIEUR JAUNE ET BLEU" 1946

JOSEPH GRANIÉ "MARGUERITE MORENO"

RECORD COMPANY VEGA, COLLECTION "LES CONCERTS DU DOMAINE MUSICAL" STRAVINSK · AGON, GIACOMETT

DENYS PUECH BEAUTIFUL "AURORE" SCULPTURE 1900 OF HAIR

SONIA DELAUNAY

Tête dans une Sphère-fleur
— ODILLE REDON

mais pas si lourde...
jeune fille endormie

D'ORSAY

BUECHNER'S BOY & MONET'S "COIN D'APPARTEMENT" ZHANG HUAN "FAMILY TREE"

POMPIDOU

the sky is red and i am watching it grow darker purple cloud green ribbon of sky blue at the top the tour d'eiffel.

and only the roof in topsi between us. us.

GIACOMETTI

van gogh is all blue and gold me.

idea: movie shot only of reflections —elevators, glasson paintings...)

man sleeping in the museum

BRASSAÏ "LA MAGIE" FROM IT

GORGEOUS OUTLINE MANET "GEORGES CLEMENCEAU"

L'opéra in the floor of the Musée D'orsay
→ ALSO SHADOW BOXES OF STAGE SETS FOR DON CARLOS & TRAVIATTA

"You know the word for turkey in french, it kind of sounds like dunderheads- 'cause that's what those birds are..." southern gentleman in the Degas room Nov6.

A BIT EXAGGERATE KNOPFF "L'ENCENS"

BONNARD

KUPKA "PLANS PAR COULEURS"

14.11.07
↓
15.11.07

CRAZY LOOSE LAUTREC + LOUIS BOUGLÉ

LUCIEN LÉVY-DHURMER "LA FEMME à la MÉDAILLE" ~ MYSTÈRE

LACOSTE - LA MAIN DOMBRE...

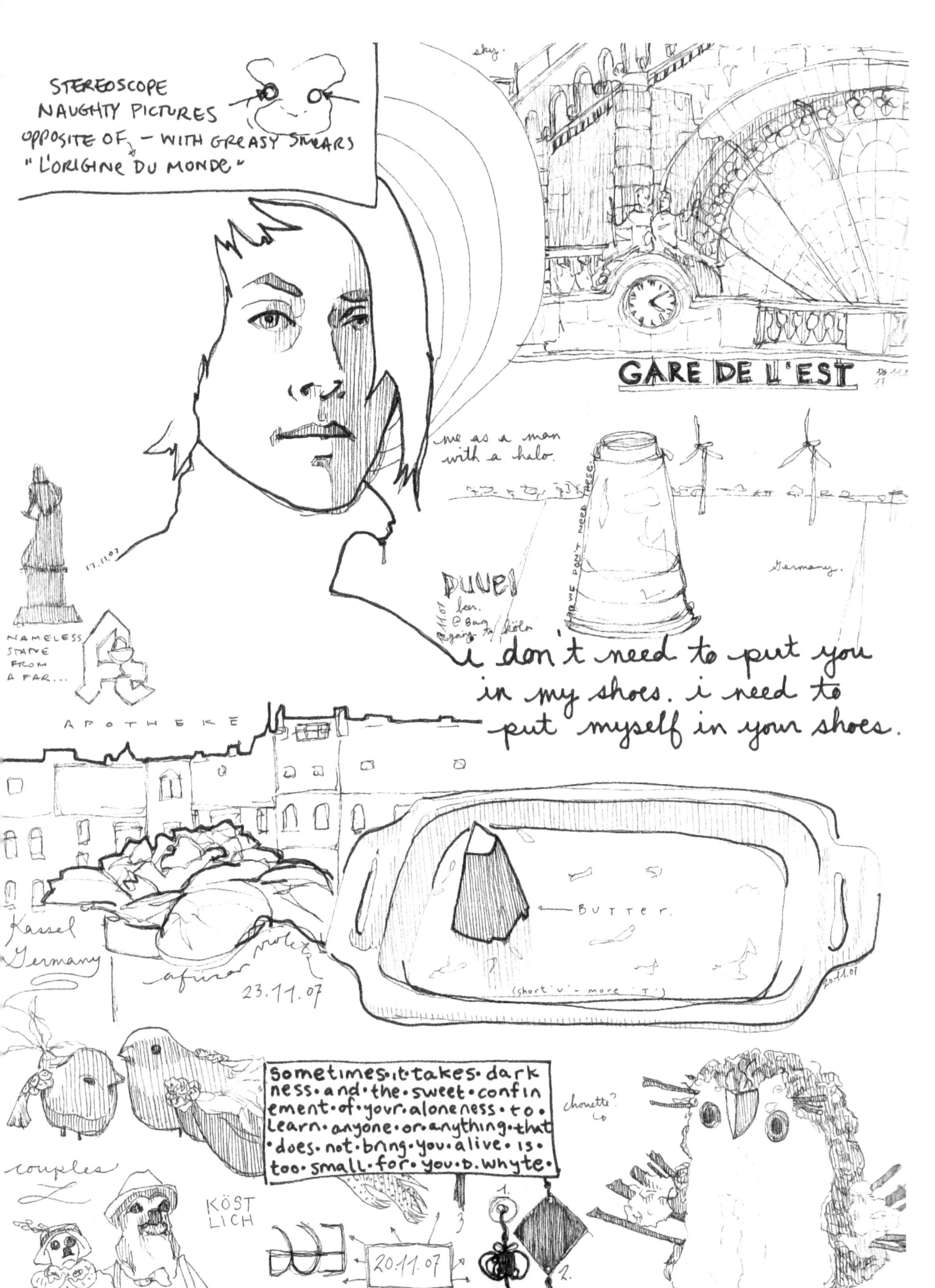

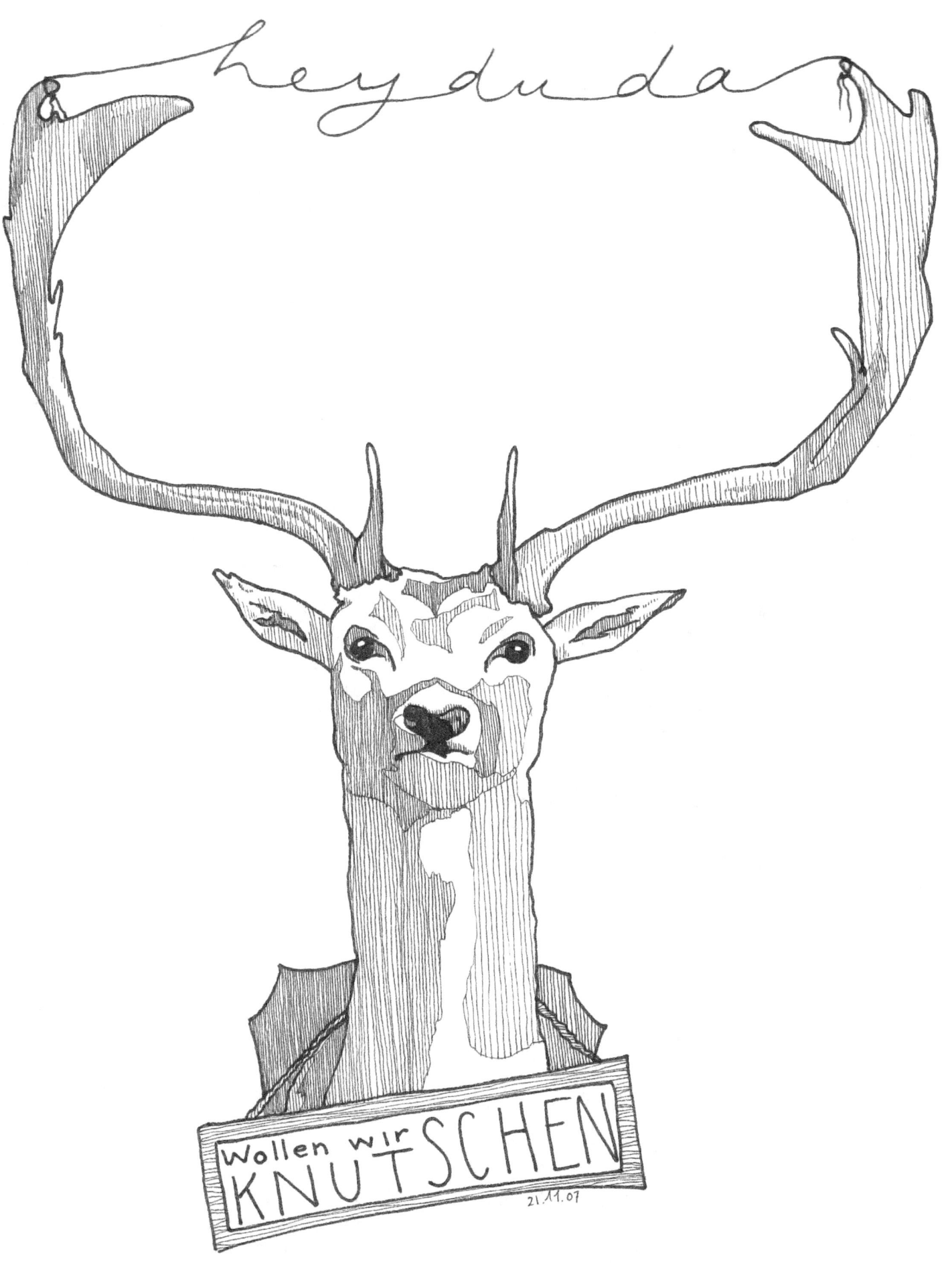

Mnemotechnics...

PAGE 78
MIDDLE TP

"Lucy was thinking: If I keep telling myself that I know exactly where I'm going and exactly who I want to see — then nobody will stop me."

The Iron Woman by Ted Hughes

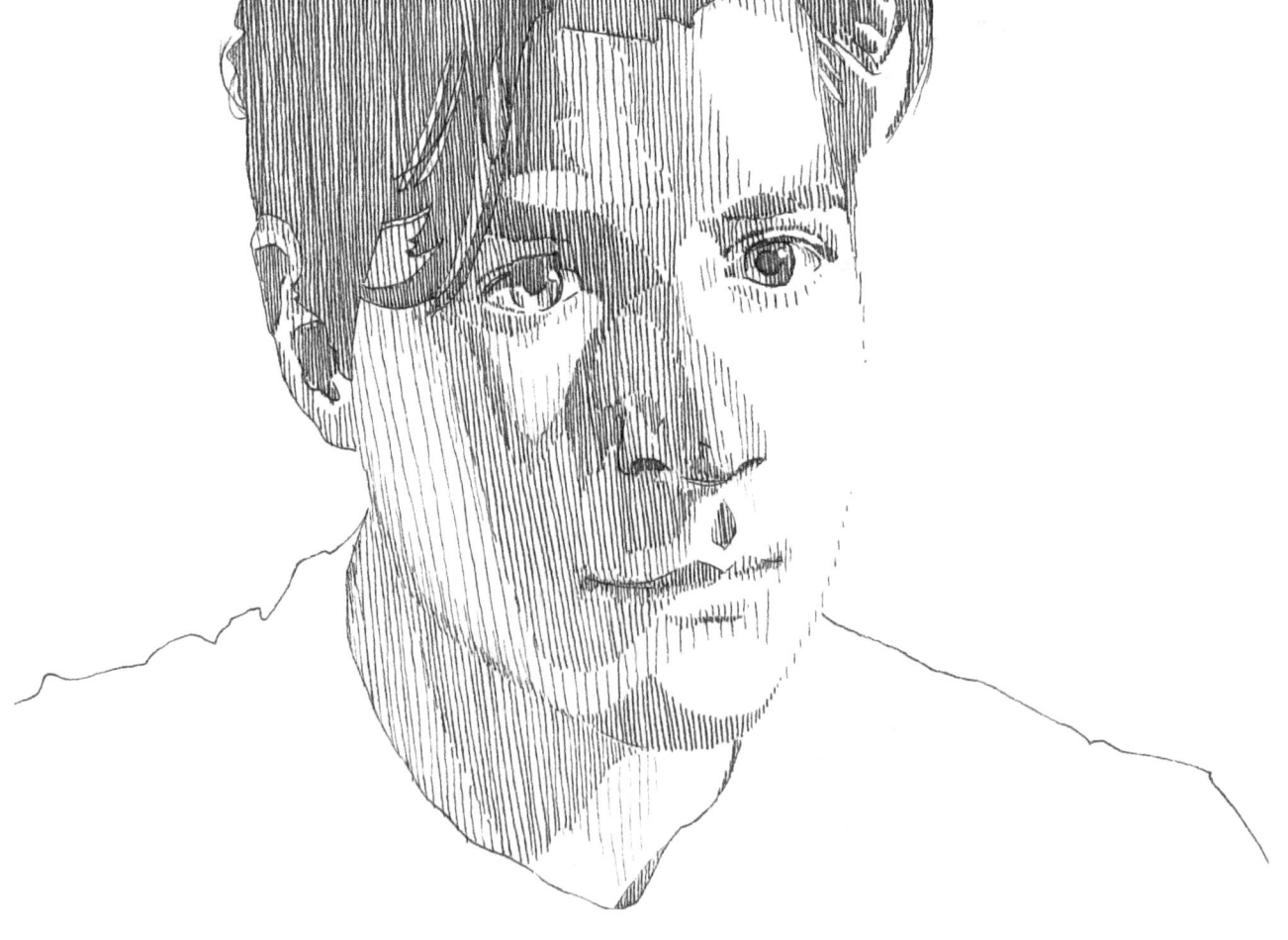

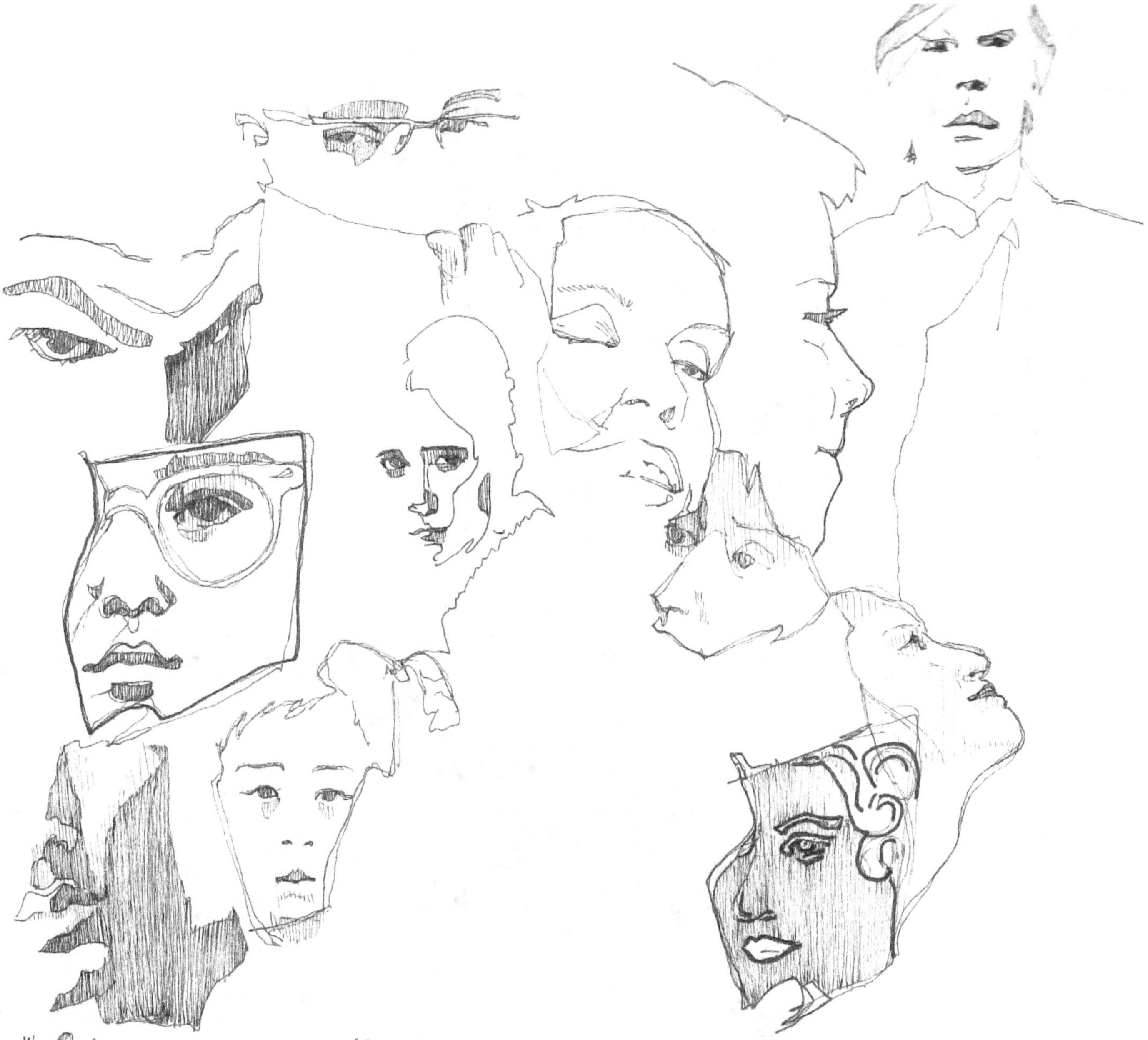

"Perhaps a man really dies when his brain stops, when he loses the power to take in a new idea .... wonderfully learned, wonderfully good taste — but he's not capable of change."
Coming up for air -George Orwell

Deutungslos...

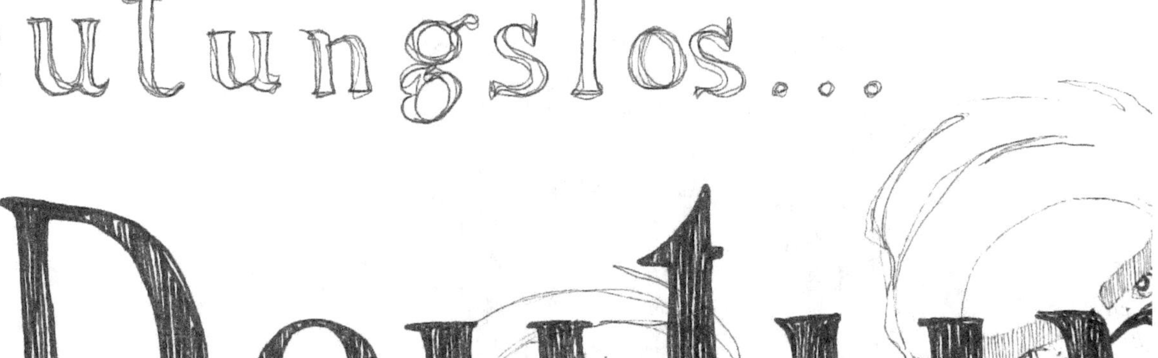

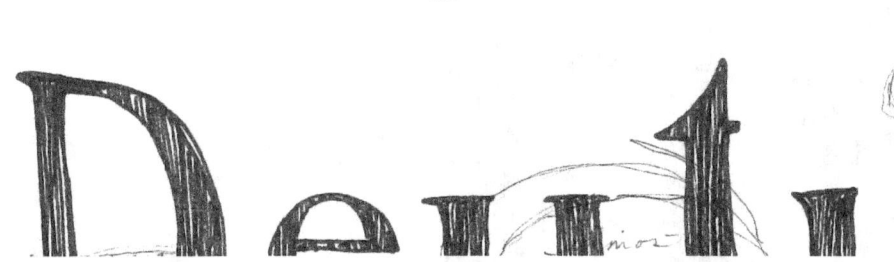
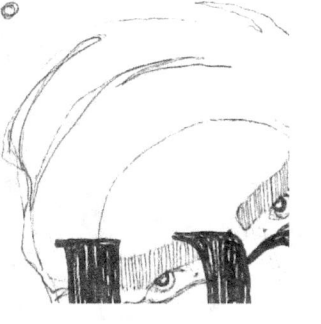

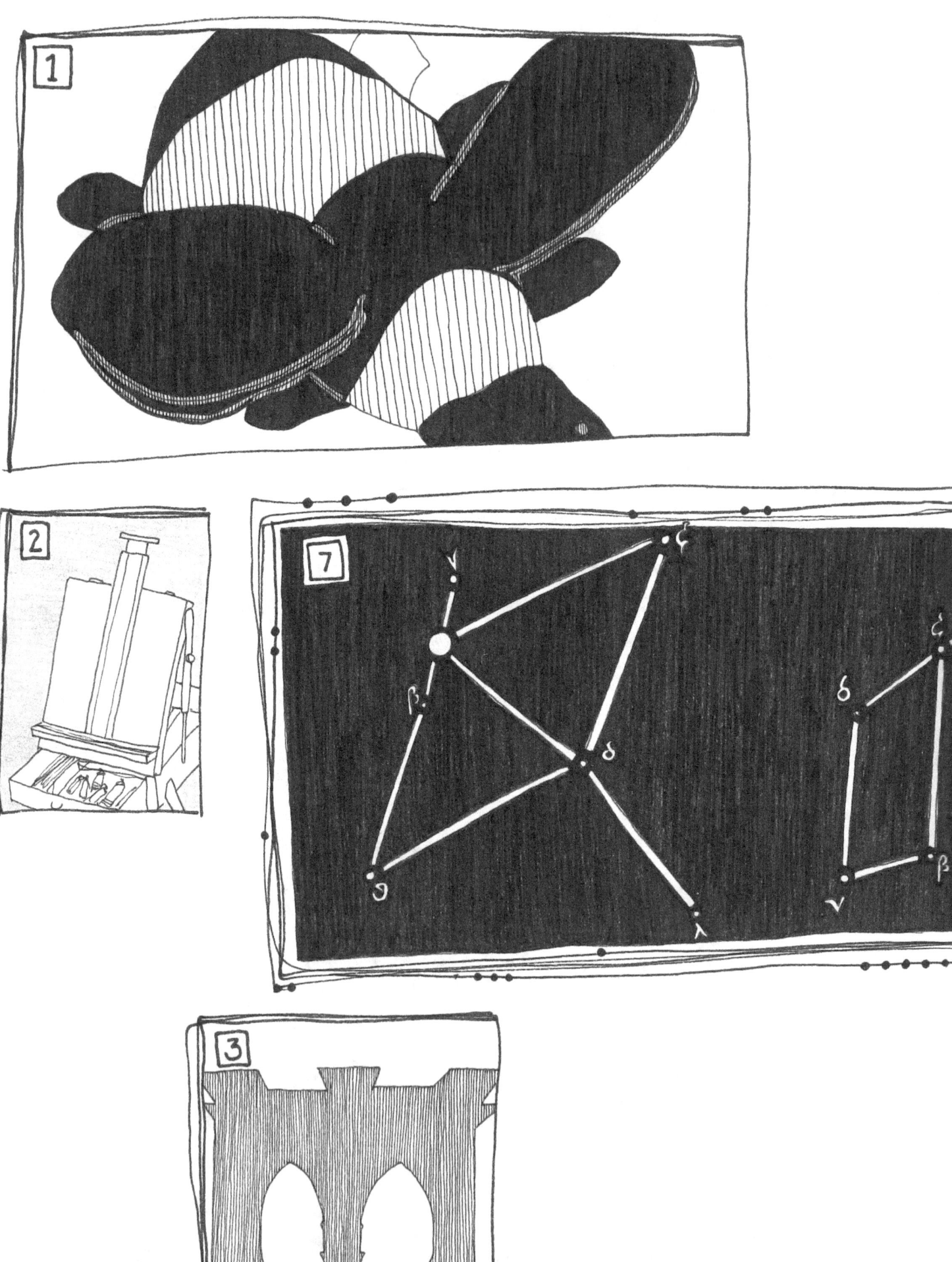

4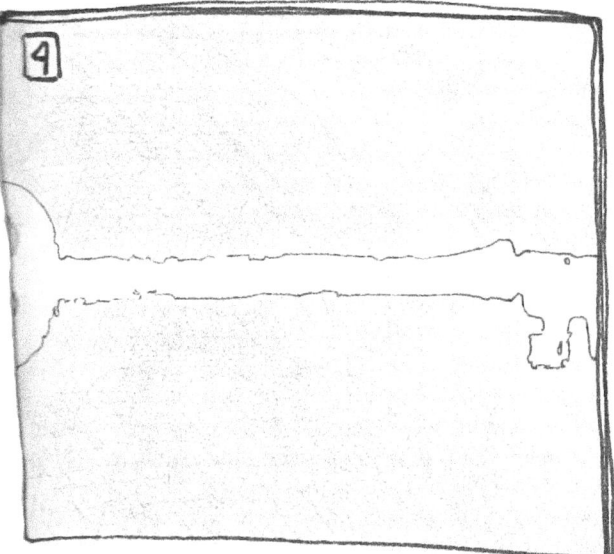

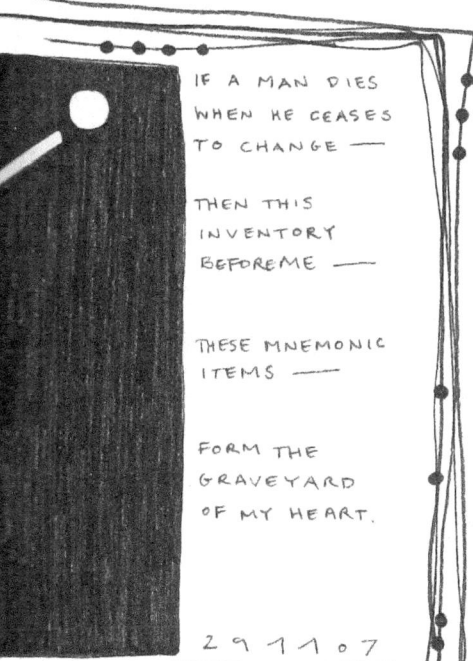

IF A MAN DIES
WHEN HE CEASES
TO CHANGE ——

THEN THIS
INVENTORY
BEFOREME ——

THESE MNEMONIC
ITEMS ——

FORM THE
GRAVEYARD
OF MY HEART.

2 9 1 1 0 7

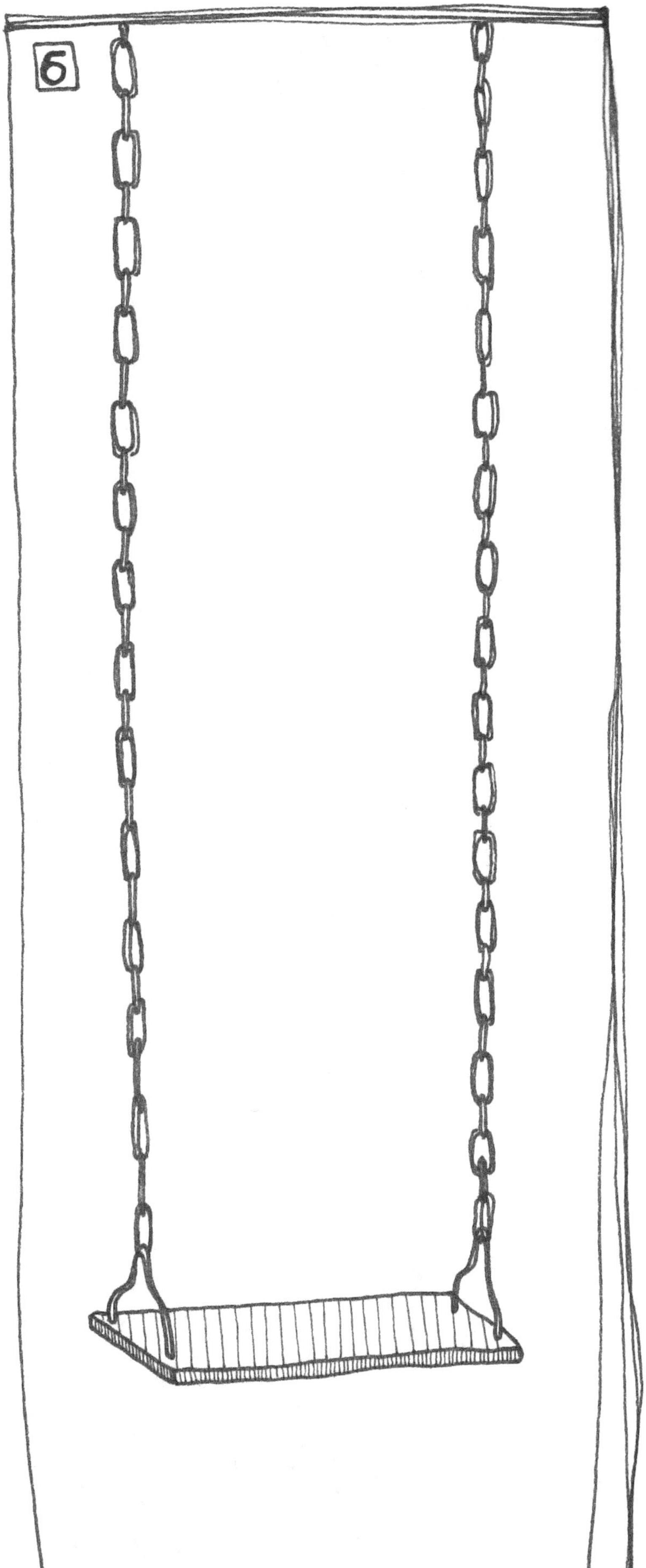

5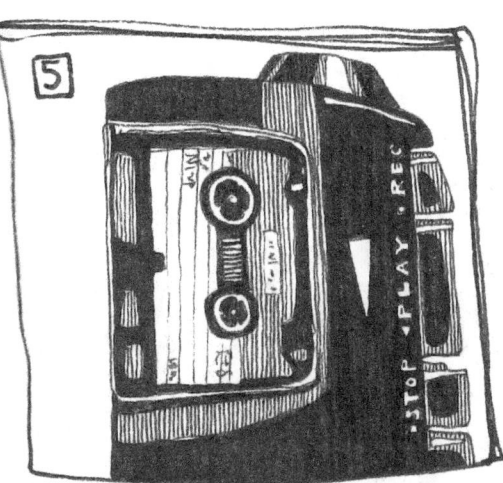

6

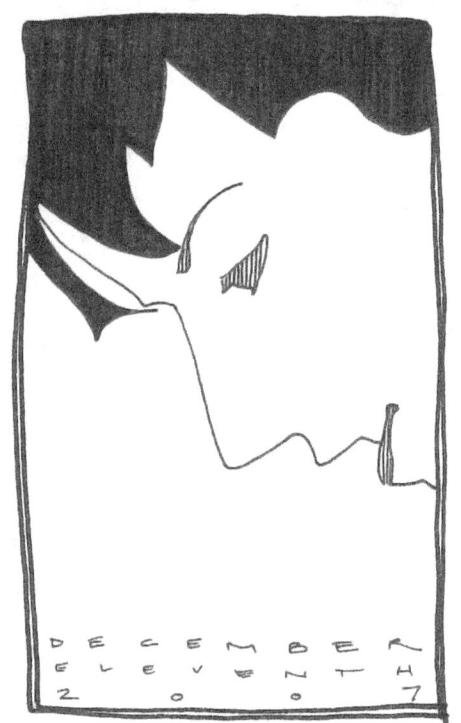

DECEMBER ELEVENTH 2007

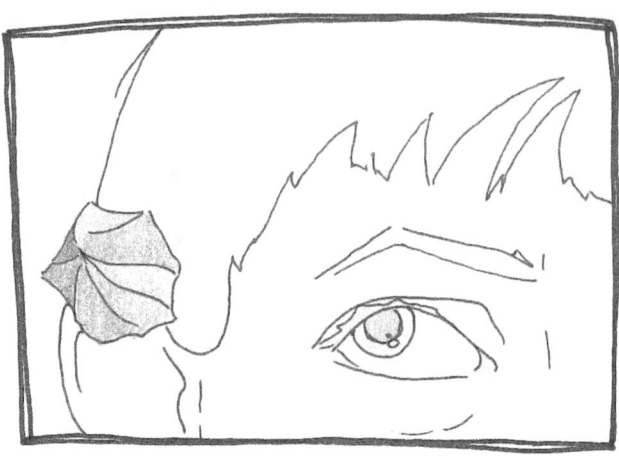

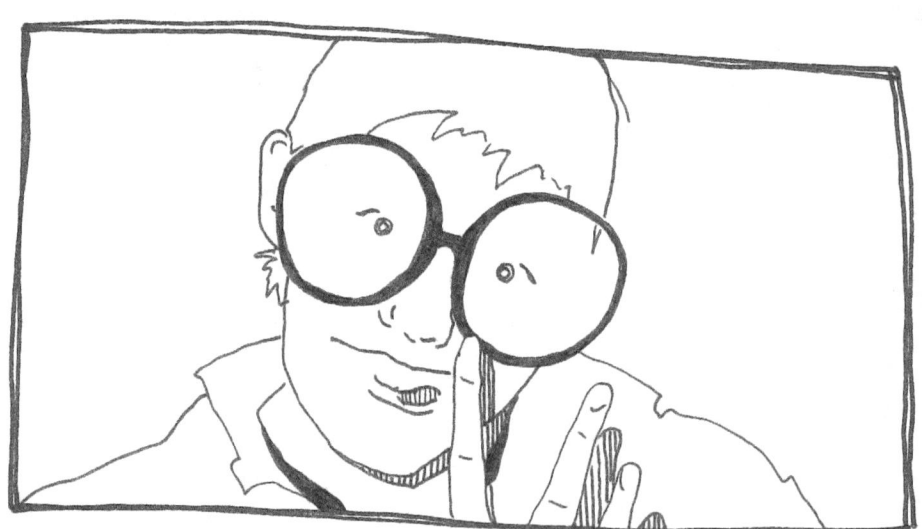

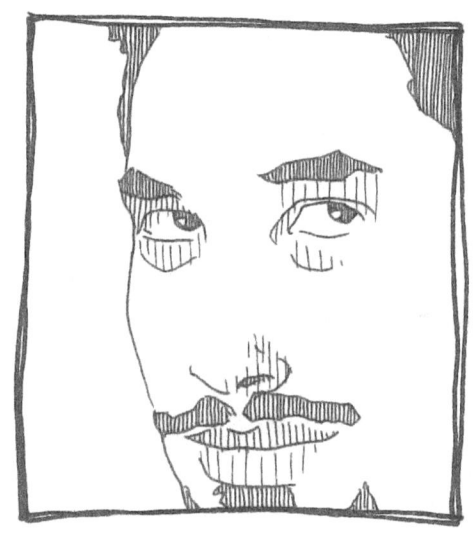

NEW YORK CITY

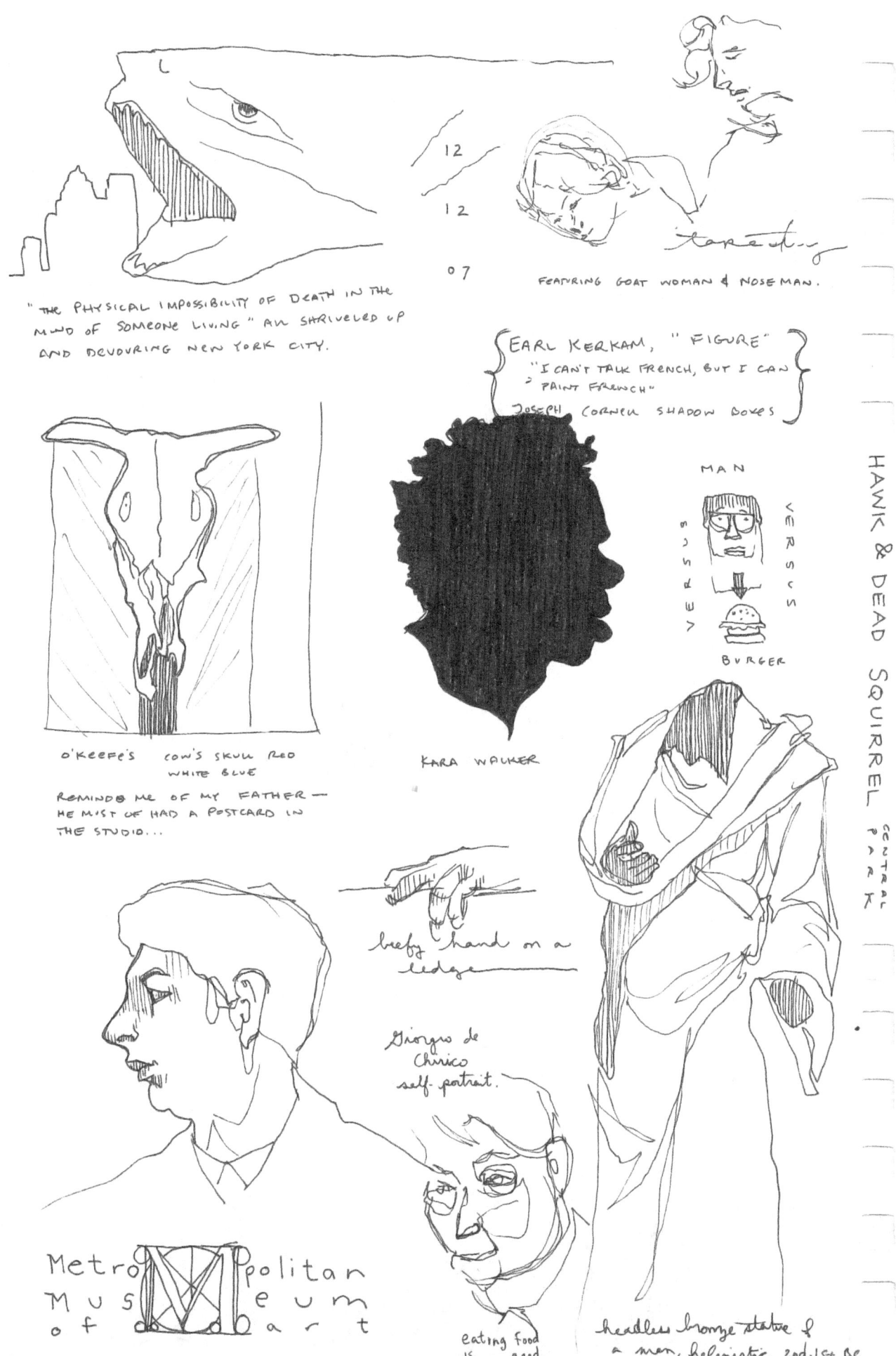

"THE PHYSICAL IMPOSSIBILITY OF DEATH IN THE
MIND OF SOMEONE LIVING" ALL SHRIVELED UP
AND DEVOURING NEW YORK CITY.

12

12

07

FEATURING GOAT WOMAN & NOSE MAN.

{ EARL KERKAM, "FIGURE"
"I CAN'T TALK FRENCH, BUT I CAN
PAINT FRENCH"
JOSEPH CORNELL SHADOW BOXES }

MAN
VERSUS
VERSUS
VERSUS
BURGER

O'KEEFE'S   COW'S SKULL RED
WHITE BLUE

KARA WALKER

REMINDS ME OF MY FATHER—
HE MUST OF HAD A POSTCARD IN
THE STUDIO...

beefy hand on a
ledge

Giorgio de
Chirico
self-portrait.

HAWK & DEAD SQUIRREL CENTRAL PARK

Metropolitan
Museum
of art

eating food
is good.

headless bronze statue of
a man, helenistic 2nd-1st BC

BERND & HILLA BECHER
"WATER TOWERS"

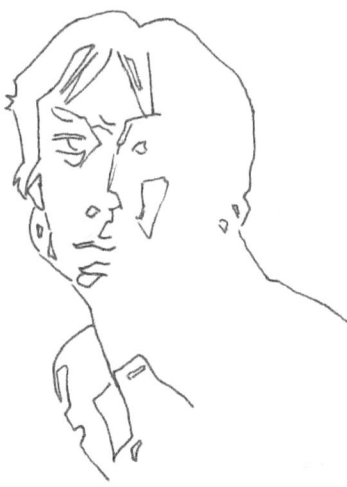

FROM SHARON LOCKHART
PHOTO, "UNTITLED" 1996

- consider painting over a grisaille — like Ingres…
  it's amazing who how his portraits seem like old friends.
- degas either had a crazy memory or just got to
  be so good due to how prolific he was.
- Toulouse-lautrec and "The Englishman at the Moulin Rouge"
  the lady in the background and his maw.
- degas again — "woman on a sofa" pink paper w/ blue dress.
- manet and courbet are chameleons — I can't spell.
- Lerolle — organ rehearsal — the woman is getting eaten
  by light — her face especially. precise architecture

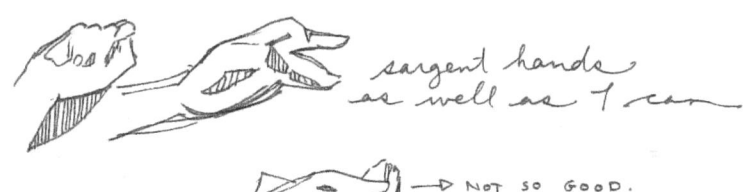

sargent hands
as well as I can

→ NOT SO GOOD.
MADE A BABY CRY.

- green venetian blinds in William Open's s.p. 1910
- Gérôme's "Pygmalion and Galatea" his hand on her left breast
  "well, on the side… very alluring — a guilty pleasure…"
- Andrea Dezsö, "Lessons from my mother 2005-6"
  "my mother claimed that our nanny had six puppy dogs
  sewn into her stomach by her previous employer."

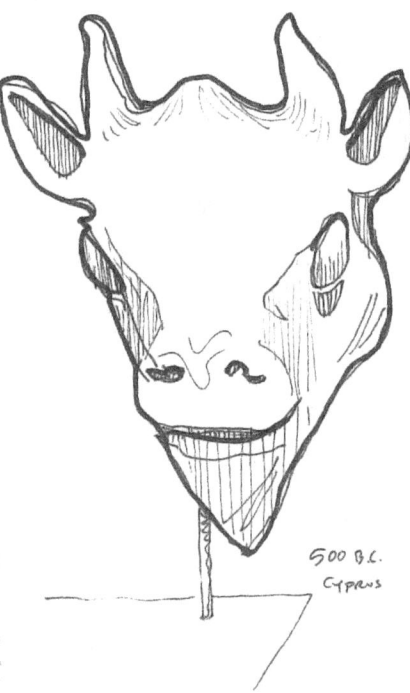

500 B.C.
CYPRUS

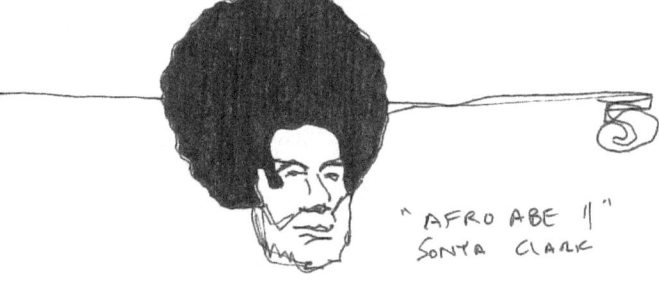

"AFRO ABE II"
SONYA CLARK

- Paul Villinski — "Lament" lost gloves found in the streets
  sewn together with blue thread into a pair of wings.
- Shizuko Kimura — "Models in New York 2006 — drawing in
  thread on gossamer fabric… just gorgeous, no words.
- enjoyed going from tapely exhibit in the Met
  to a contemporary "tapestry" (more like embroidery)
  show at the Museum of American Craft… I think…
- Alex Trebek had a heart attack! Read on the subway!

BUT TODAY IS DEC. 12. 2007.
CLOUDRAG ISSUE No. 2 RELEASE
IN PORTLAND, OR. I AM IN N.Y.C.

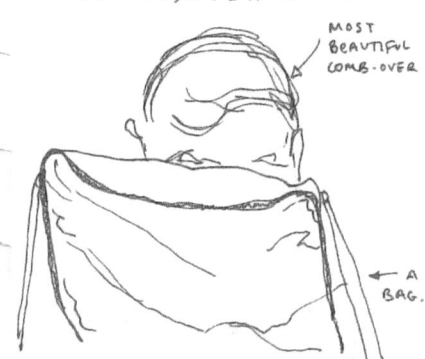

MOST
BEAUTIFUL
COMB-OVER

← A
BAG.

A
HAT.

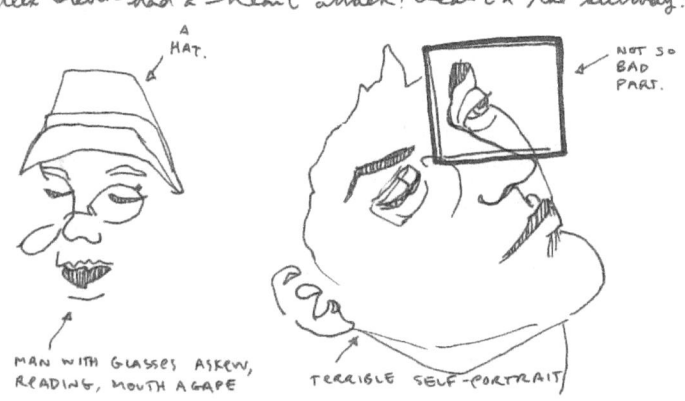

NOT SO
BAD
PART.

MAN WITH GLASSES ASKEW,
READING, MOUTH AGAPE

TERRIBLE SELF-PORTRAIT

oh millie, oh millie...

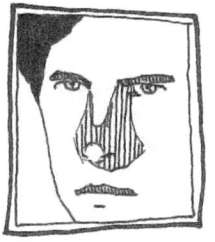 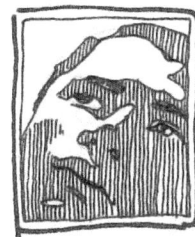 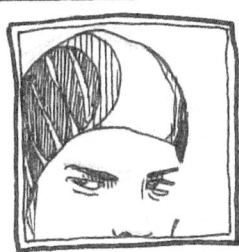 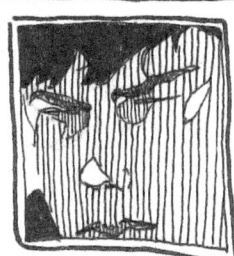

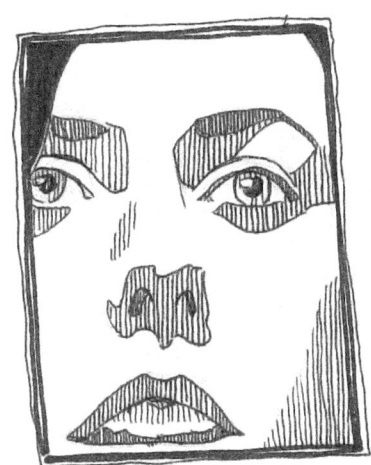

there are millions of men.

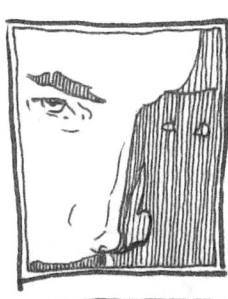 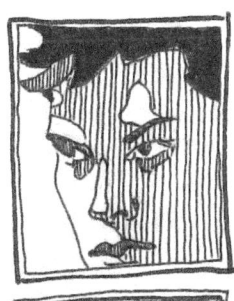 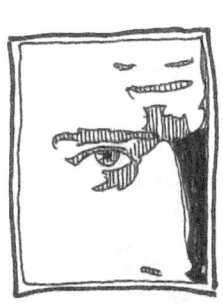 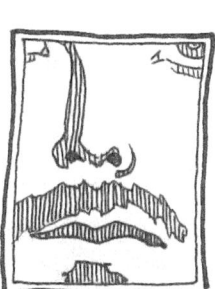

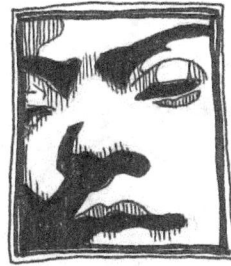 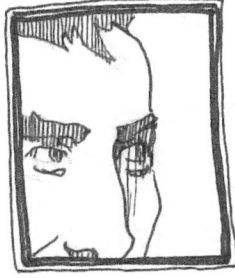 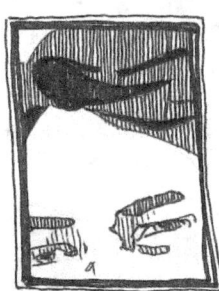 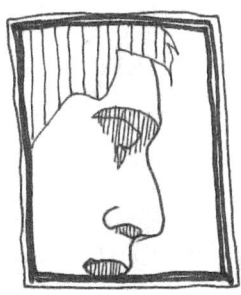

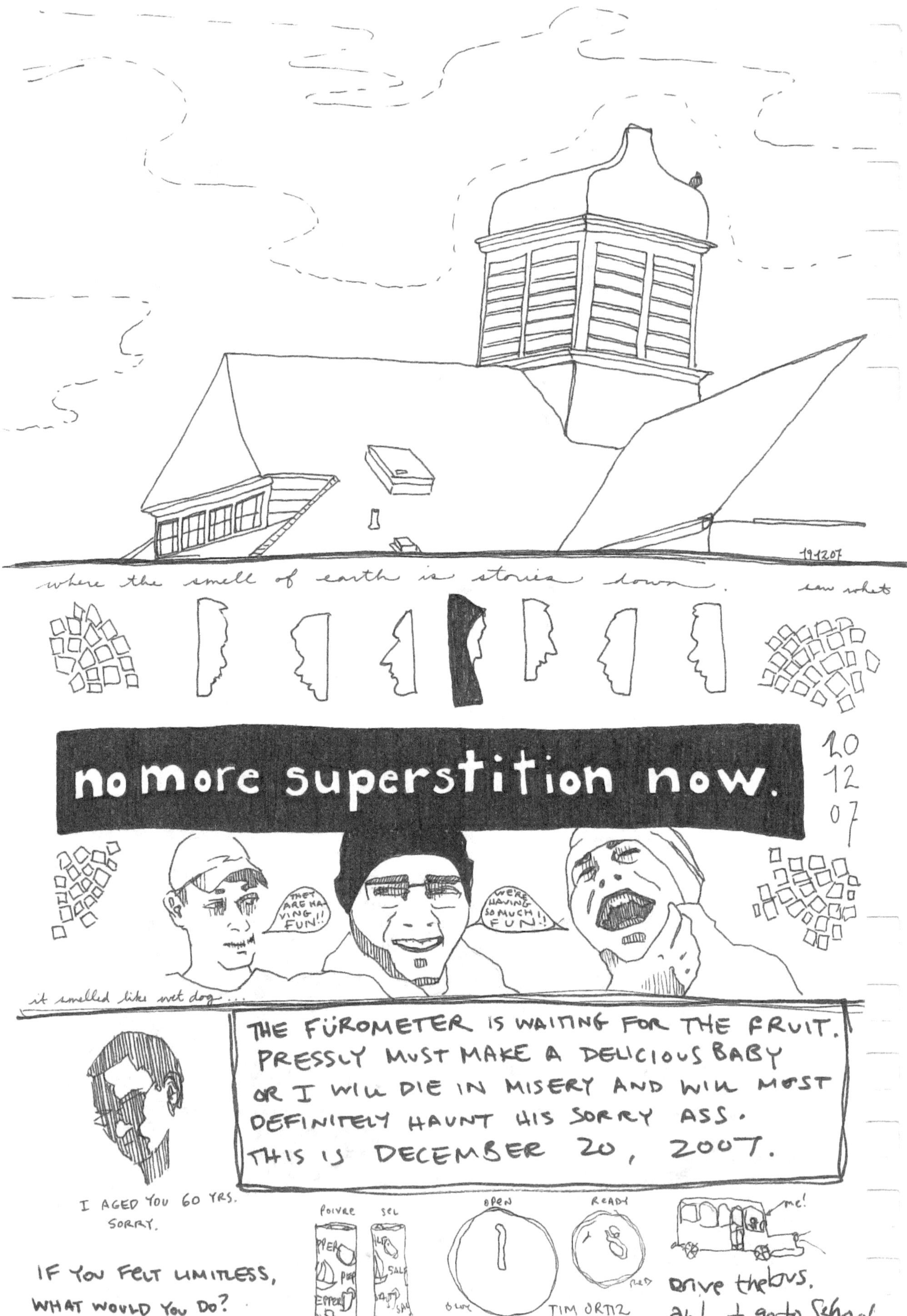

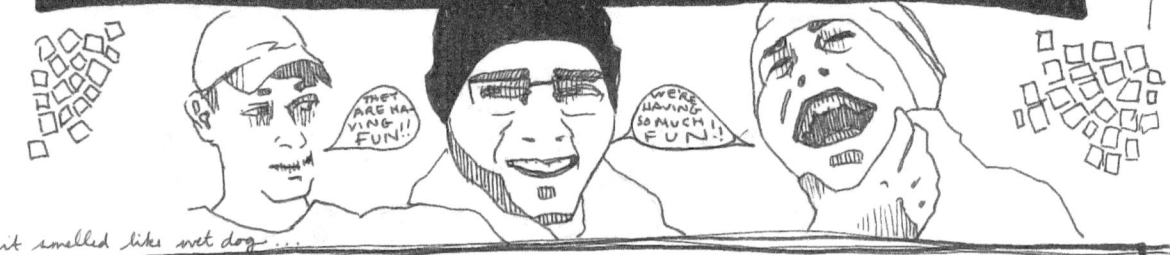

where the smell of earth is stories down.

eau sakets

no more superstition now.

20
12
07

THEY ARE HAVING FUN!!

WE'RE HAVING SO MUCH FUN!!

it smelled like wet dog ...

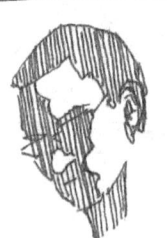

THE FÜROMETER IS WAITING FOR THE FRUIT.
PRESSLY MUST MAKE A DELICIOUS BABY
OR I WILL DIE IN MISERY AND WILL MOST
DEFINITELY HAUNT HIS SORRY ASS.
THIS IS DECEMBER 20, 2007.

I AGED YOU 60 YRS.
SORRY.

IF YOU FELT LIMITLESS,
WHAT WOULD YOU DO?

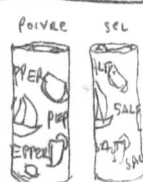
POIVRE   SEL

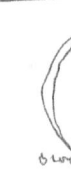

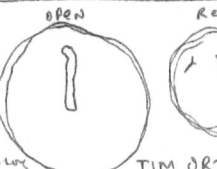
OPEN   READY

TIM ORTIZ

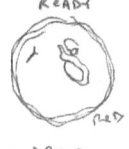

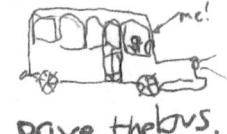
me!

Drive the bus.
and not go to school.

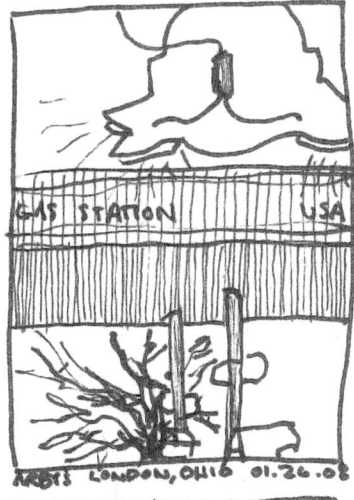

GAS STATION   USA

NDT'S LONDON, OHIO 01.26.08

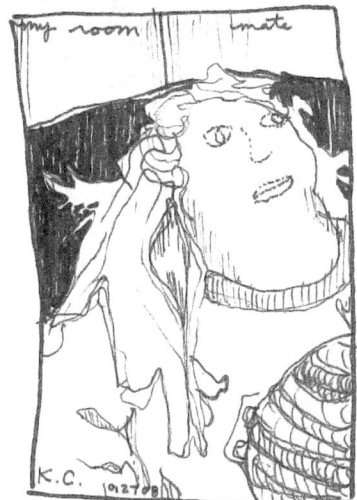

my room   mate

K.C. 01.27.08

MAJOR GENERAL JOSHUA CHAMBERLAIN

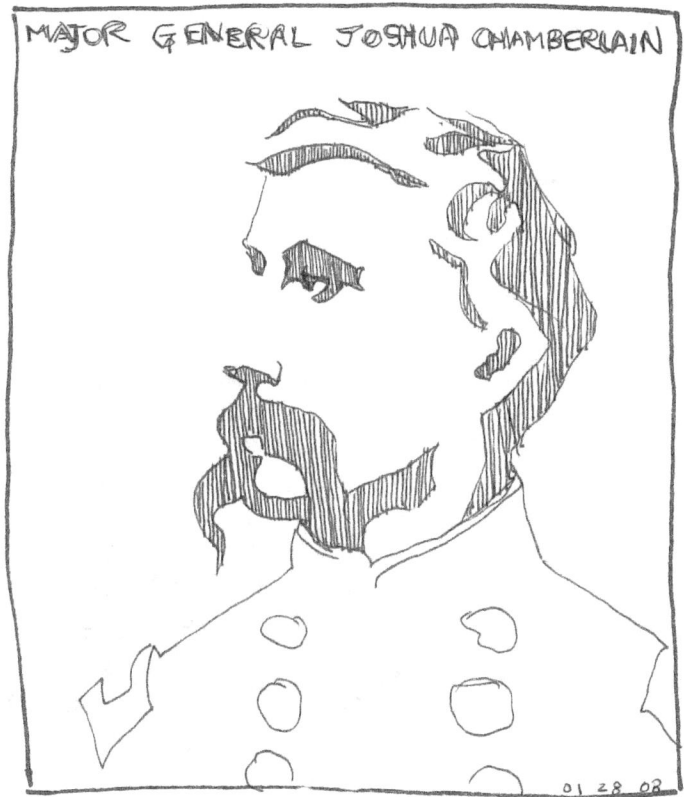

01 28 08

I played Pennsylvania Polka in Pa and it felt so right. My favorite moment so far in the trip.

"IT'S A BRAIN WITH A TOOTH, LIQUID ~~EYES~~ TISSUE, AND A COUPLE OF EYES" BRANDY   BLOOMINGTON, IN

FK-BRADV

GATOR

01.26-27.08

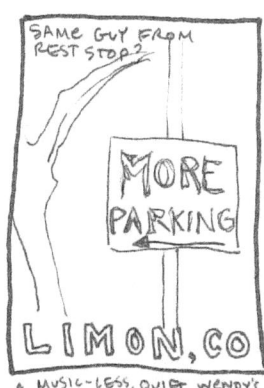

SAME GUY FROM REST STOP?

MORE PARKING

LIMON, CO

A MUSIC-LESS, QUIET WENDY'S

"HELLO"

01   2 8   08

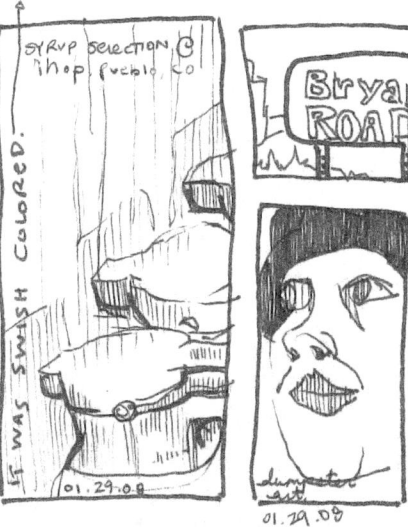

SYRUP SELECTION @ iHop, Pueblo, CO

I'm thinking about FLOURIDE MOUTH WASH. IT WAS SWISH COLORED.

01.29.08

Brya ROAD

dungeon it

01.29.08

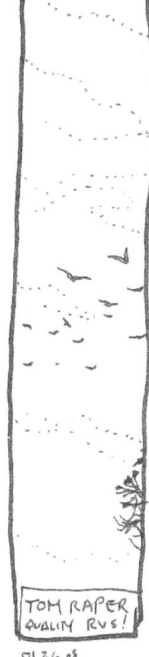

TOM RAPER QUALITY RVS!

01 26 08

THIS IS GOING PRETTY WELL SO FAR. WE ESTABLISHED EARLY ON; THE NIGHT BEFORE I LEPT, THAT YOU ARE NOT IN LOVE WITH ME AND THEN I REALIZED BY SAYING THAT I WAS STILL IN LOVE WITH YOU THAT I WASN'T ANYMORE. IT'S FUNNY HOW SOMETIMES THE ACT OF SAYING SOMETHING THAT HAS BEEN KICKING AROUND IN YOUR BRAIN ALL CONFLICTEDLY WILL LET YOU REALLY KNOW ONE WAY OR THE OTHER WITH UTMOST CERTAINTY. SO MY BREAKFAST IS HERE I SHOULD EAT IT. IT LOOKS LIKE WAY TOO MUCH FOOD THOUGH. THERE'S THIS BUS BOY-DISHWASHER BOY HERE WHO IS REALLY INTENSE AND FUN TO WATCH. TALL AND C-SHAPED, SO FOCUSED ON WHAT HE IS DOING WALKING IN STRAIGHT LINES AND THEN PERFECTLY TURNING AROUND AND RETRACING HIS PERFECT STRAIGHT LINE PATH. IT'S SO SURREAL FOR SOME REASON. OH AND COFFEE IS SO GOOD. THE KINKS ARE PLAYING ON THE PIPED IN MUSIC SYSTEM. I HAVE A GENTLEMAN SITTING IN THE NEXT BOOTH OVER ALL OF A SUDDEN. JUST NOW. I AM STRUCK WITH WHAT I AM DOING. I'VE BEEN ON THE ROAD FOR THREE DAYS NOW. THIS IS MY FOURTH DAY - THE MIDDLE OF MY TRIP AND I HAVE TO MOVE BACK INTO FORTY AND AND THAT SCENE THERE AND I WANT TO FALL IN LOVE WITH SOMEONE WHO IS IN LOVE WITH ME. BUT ONLY EVENTUALLY.

01.29.08 PUEBLO, CO

BLINK PLEASE.

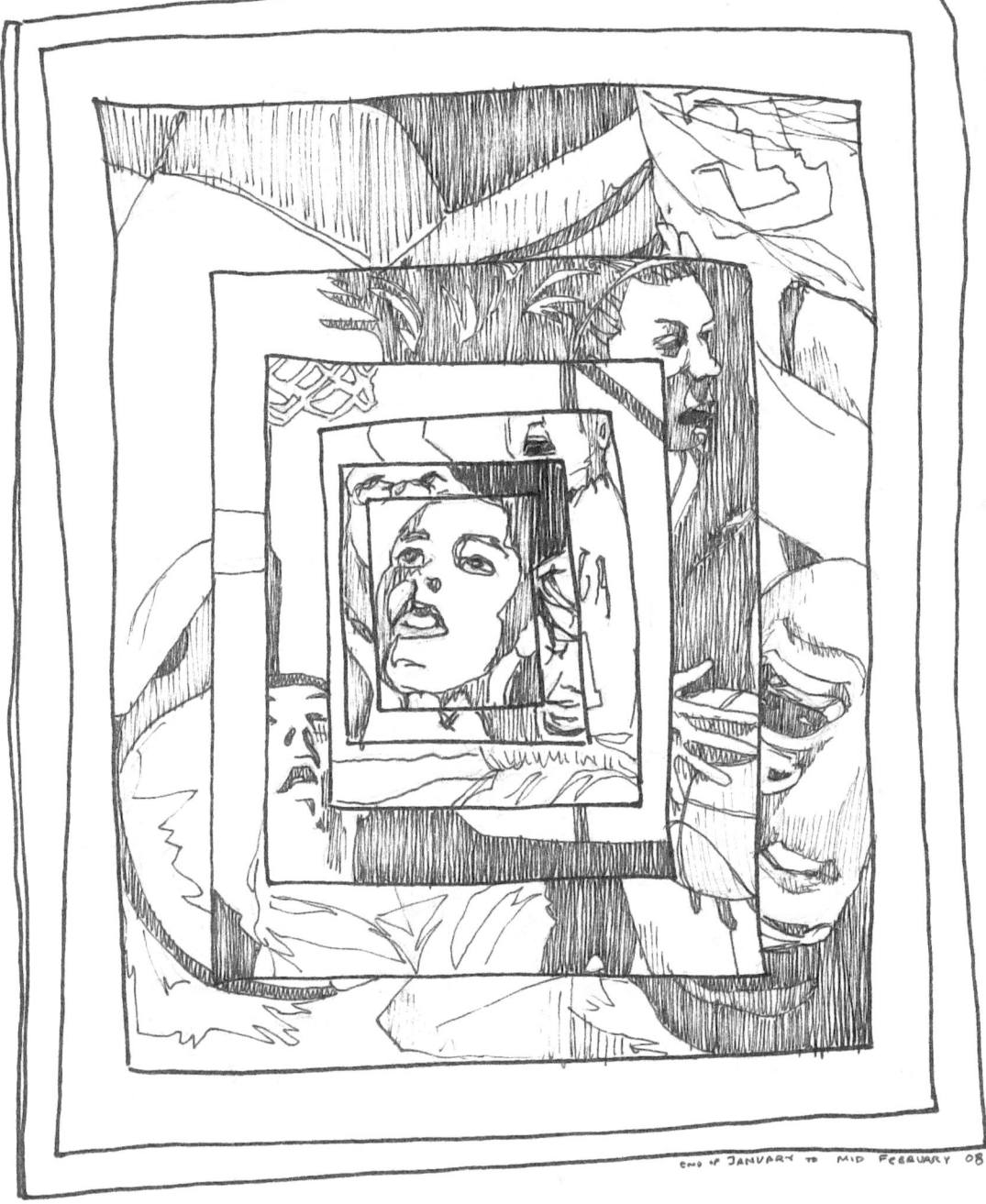

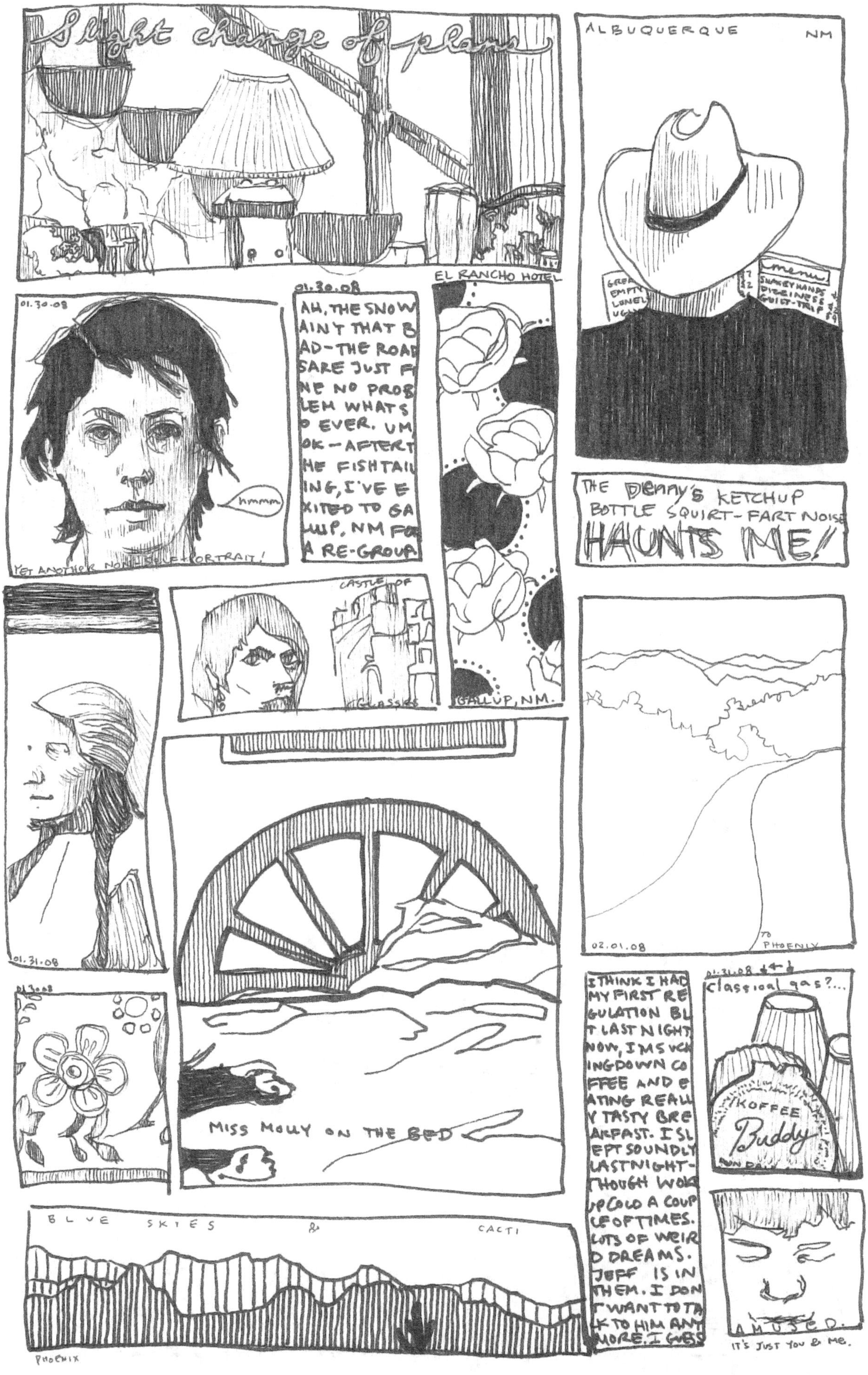

Slight change of plans

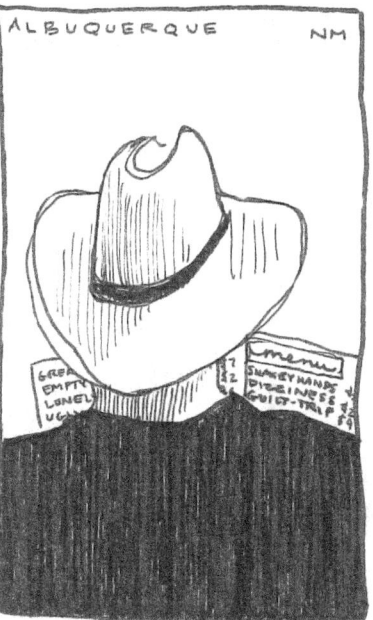

EL RANCHO HOTEL

01.30.08

AH, THE SNOW AIN'T THAT B AD – THE ROAD SARE JUST FI NE NO PROB LEM WHATS O EVER. UM OK – AFTER T HE FISHTAIL ING, I'VE E XITED TO GA LLUP, NM FOR A RE-GROUP

hmmm

YET ANOTHER NON-HL SELF-PORTRAIT!

01.30.08

CASTLE OF

GLASSES

GALLUP, NM.

THE DENNY'S KETCHUP BOTTLE SQUIRT-FART NOISE **HAUNTS ME!!**

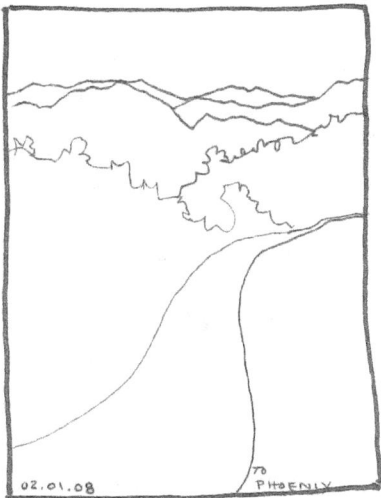

02.01.08   TO PHOENIX

01.31.08

MISS MOLLY ON THE BED

01.30.08

I THINK I HAD MY FIRST RE GULATION BL T LAST NIGHT NOW, I'M S VCK ING DOWN CO FFEE AND E ATING REALL Y TASTY BRE AKFAST. I SL EPT SOUNDLY LAST NIGHT – THOUGH WOKE UP COLD A COUP LE OF TIMES. LOTS OF WEIR D DREAMS. JEFF IS IN THEM. I DON 'T WANT TO TA LK TO HIM ANY MORE. I GUES

01.31.08 &+&   Classical gas?...

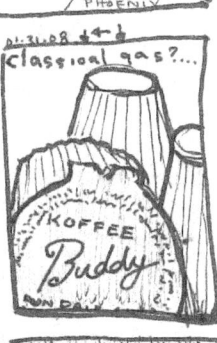

KOFFEE *Buddy*

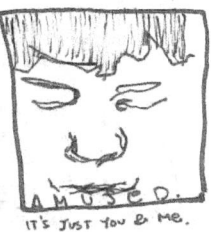

AMUSED.

IT'S JUST YOU & ME.

BLUE SKIES & CACTI

PHOENIX

02.01.08

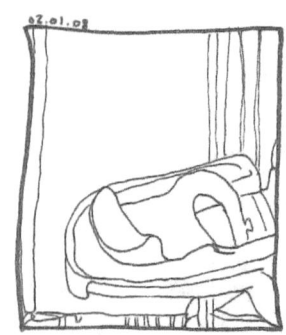

02.03.08

02.04.08

STATE PRISON

NEXT RIGHT

DO NOT
PICK UP
HITCHHIKERS

SOUTHERN CALIFORNIA

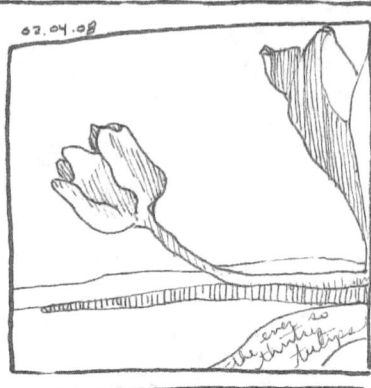

ever so
the shitting
tulips

MISS   MOLLY

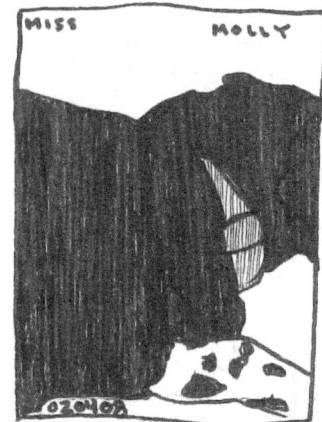

020407

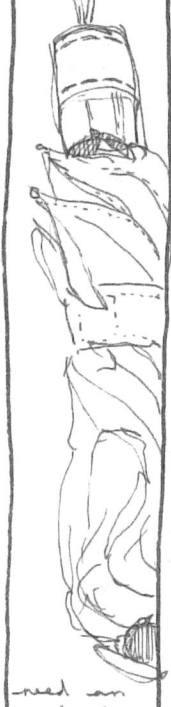

need an
umbrella
now.

020508

02.04.08

I am so so so nervous @ that kind
of nervous, when you're just about
to go on stage and perform @ you've
know you'll do fine — if you can
just calm yourself down a little bit
so, that's what I'm going through,
a nervousness that made me eat
my toast in slow motion this morn-
ing @ sigh @ it'll be all right @ I'll
find a place to stay @ I'll find
a great job @ I'll rebuild my life
from scratch — no problem... yeah

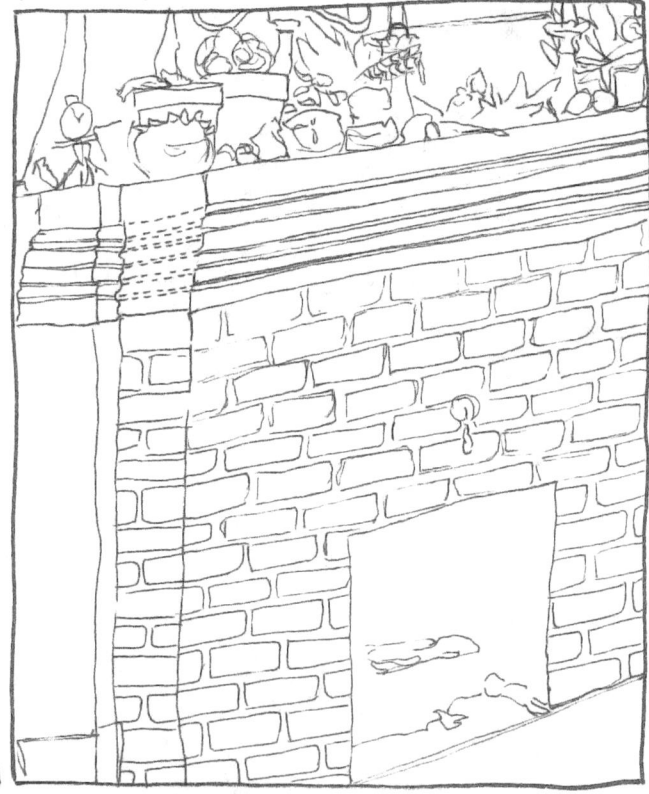

02.01.08

my new ring

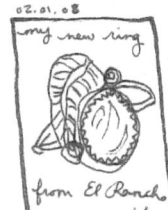

from El Rancho
I love it

02.02.08

HE'S GOT A
PILLOW OVER
YOUR FACE,
HONEY

here it comes

02.06.08

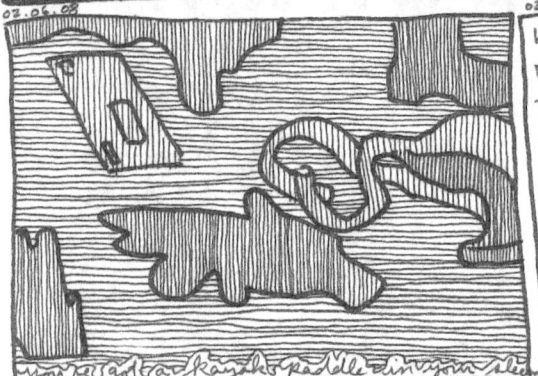

02.03.08

HE
EATS
TOAST.
WOLF
WOLF
WOLF.
HE
HAS
GILLS.

EGG SHOP.
OAKLAND.

you've got a kayak paddle in your sleep

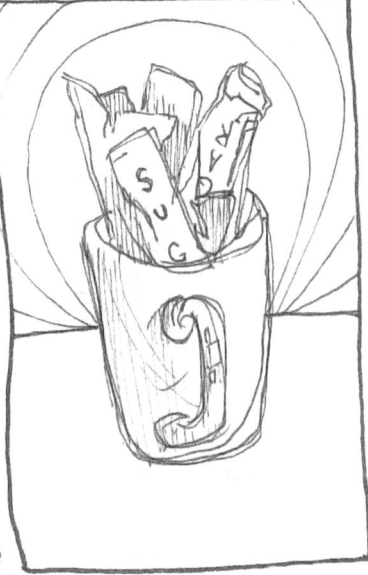

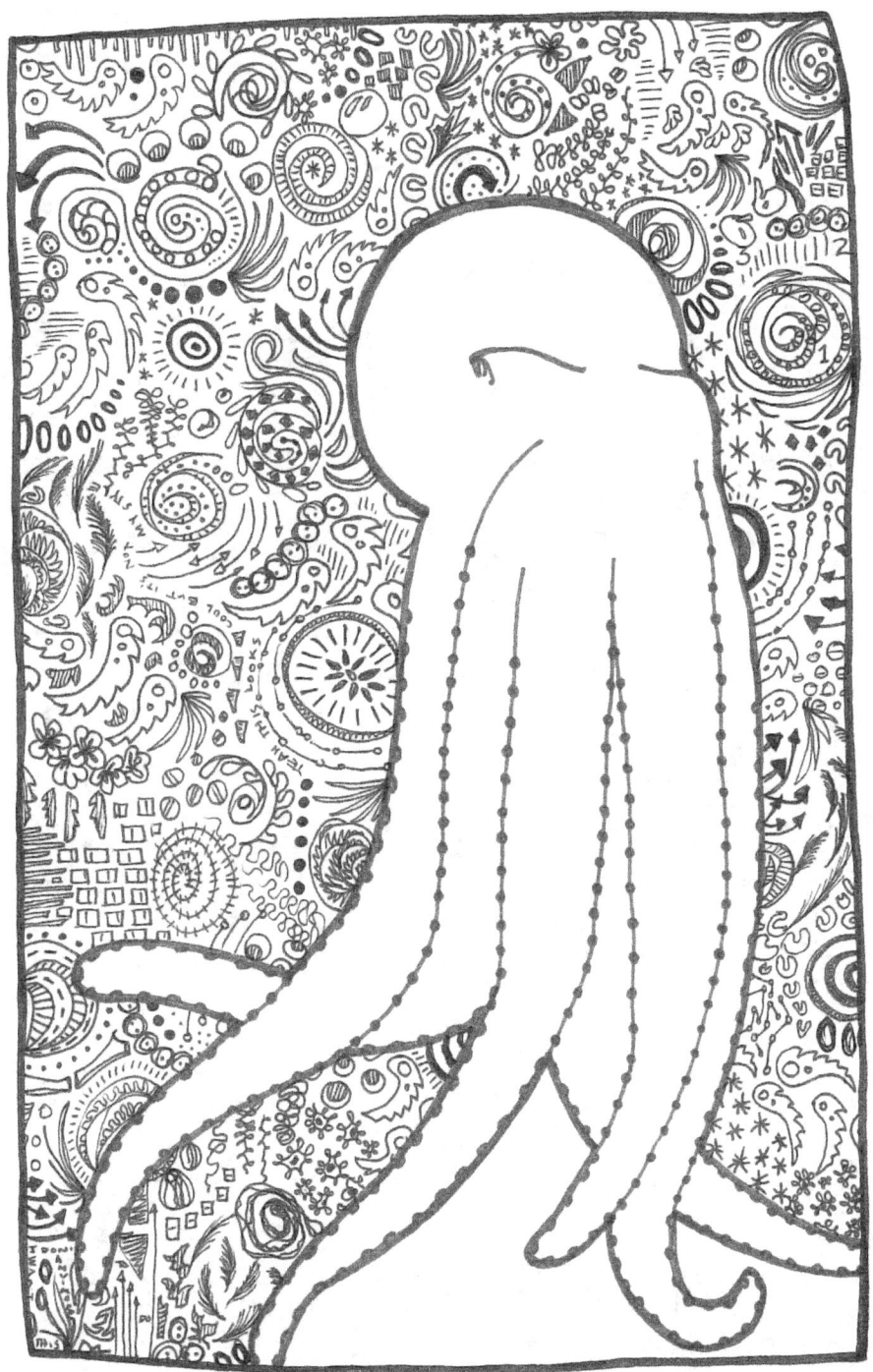

IT'S·A·BRAIN·WITH·A·TOOTH

02   09   03

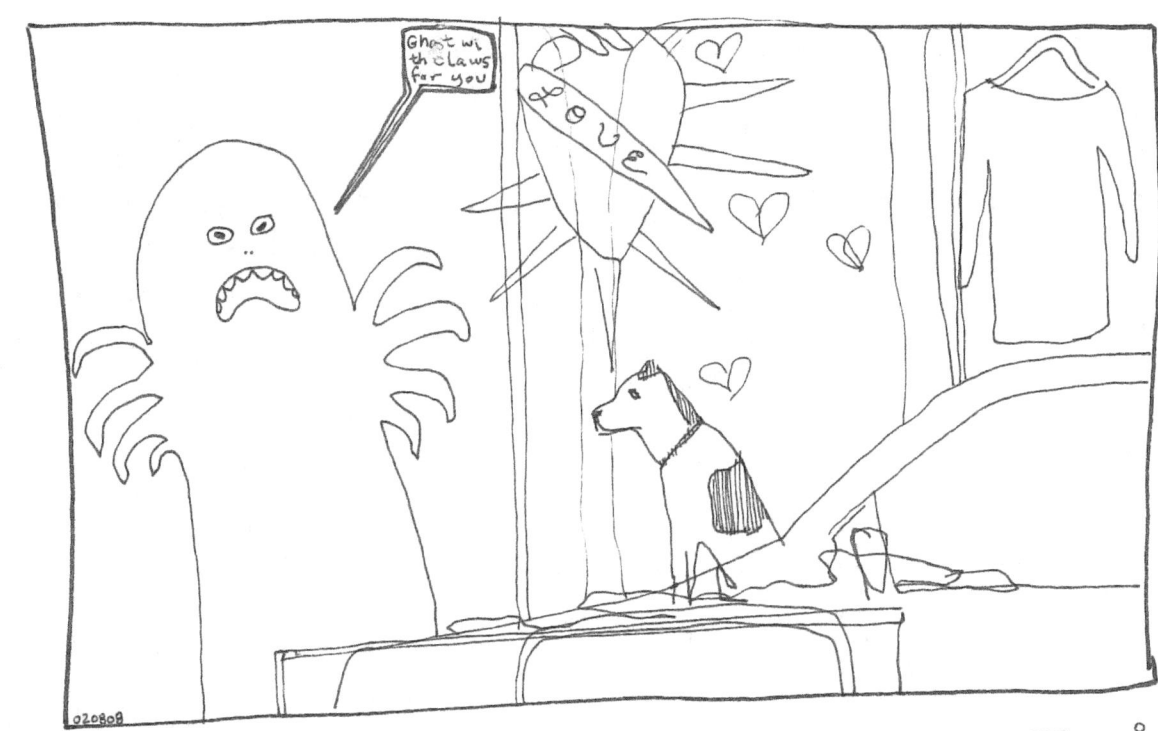

YOUR EXISTENCE gives mE
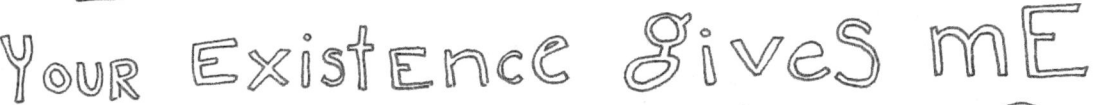

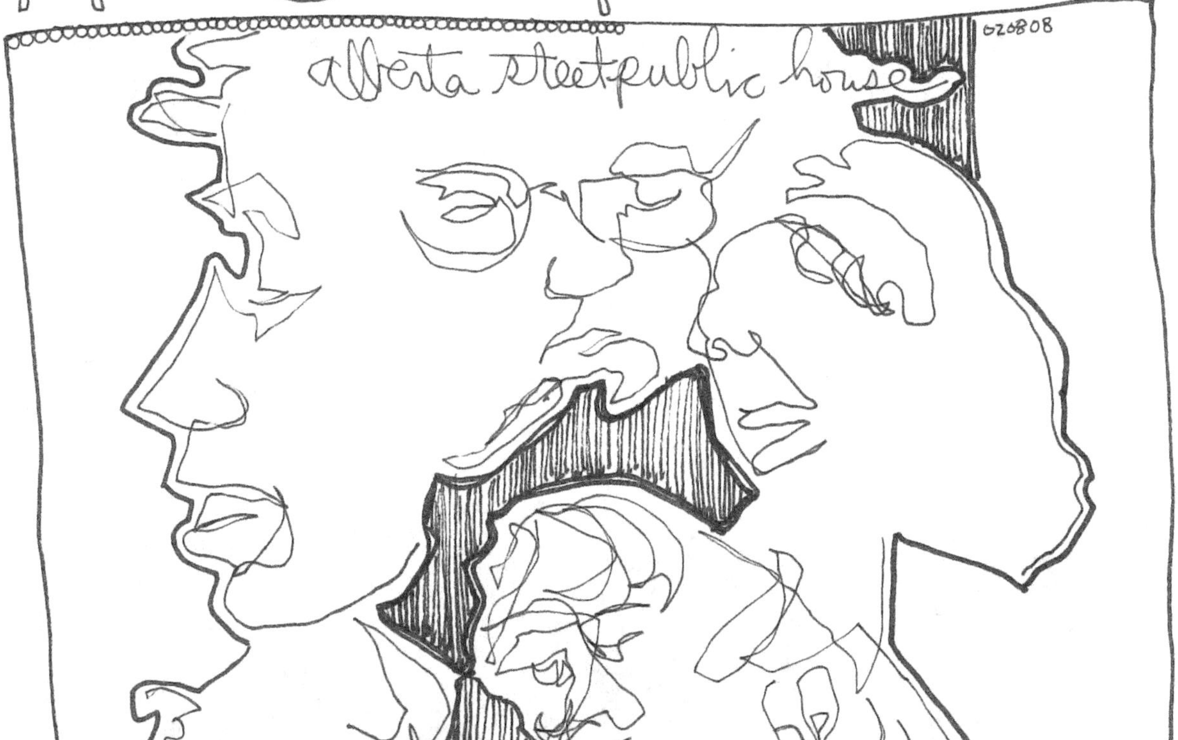

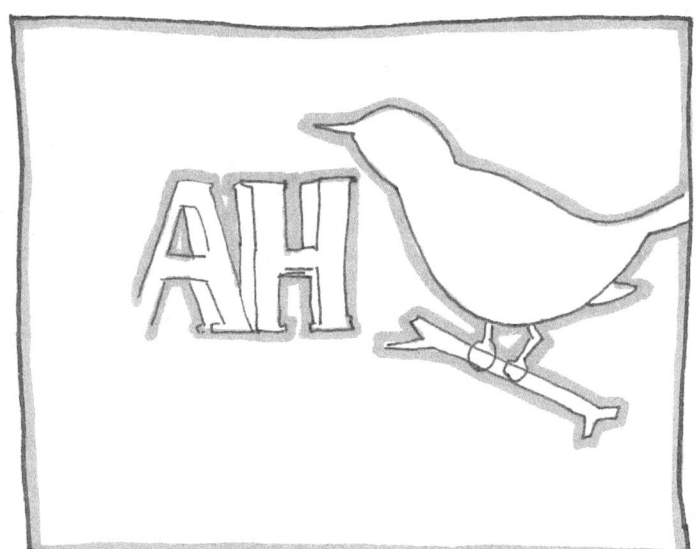

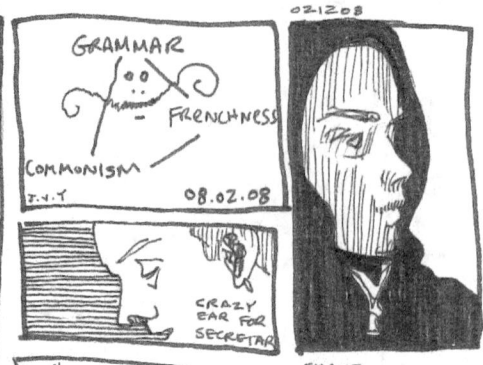

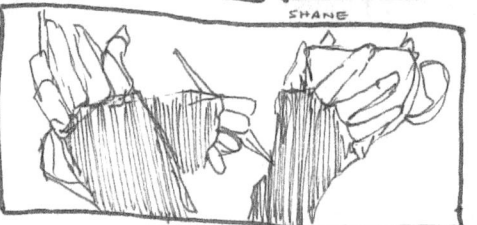

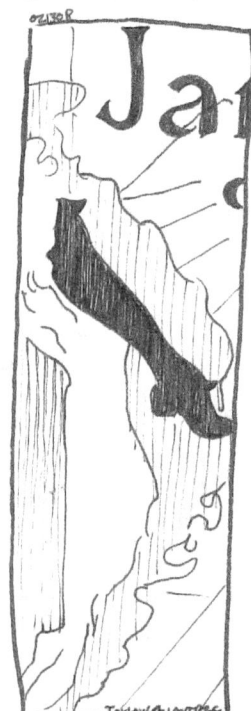

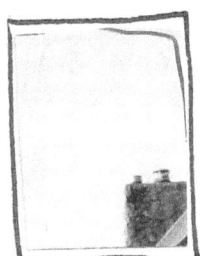

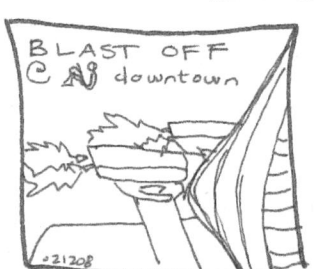

THE ODOR FROM THE FLOWER IS GONE / WHICH LIKE THY KISSES BREATHED ON ME; / THE COLOR FROM THE FLOWER IS FLOWN / WHICH GLOWED OF THEE AND ONLY THEE! A SHRIVELLED, LIFELESS VACANT FORM, / IT LIES ON MY ABANDONED BREAST; / AND MOCKS THE HEART, WHICH YET IS WARM, / WITH COLD AND SILENT REST. / I WEEP — MY TEARS REVIVE IT NOT; / I SIGH — IT BREATHES NO MORE ON ME; / ITS MUTE AND UNCOMPLAING LOT IS SUCH AS MINE SHOULD BE.

"ON A DEAD VIOLET" BY PERCY BYSSHE SHELLEY

FORGIVENESS IS THE FRAGRANCE THAT THE VIOLET SHEDS ON THE HEEL THAT HAS CRUSHED IT.

BY MARK TWAIN.

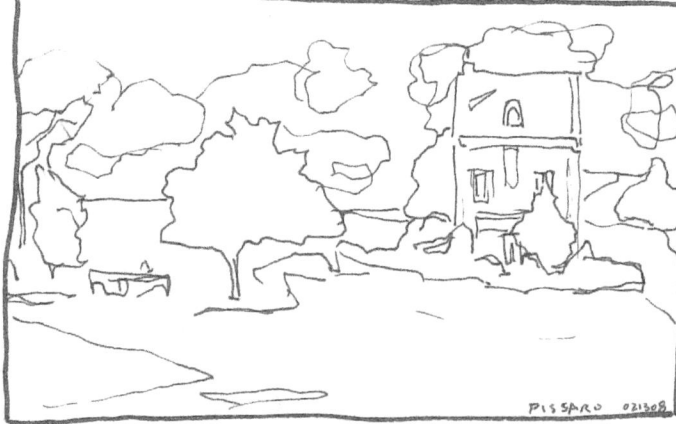

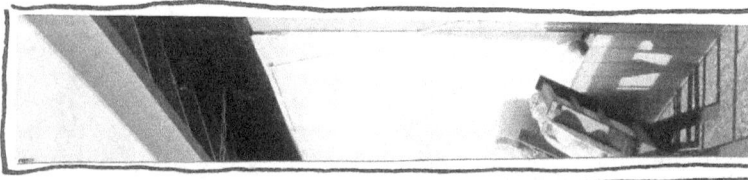

"amelia doesn't eat her food — it just slowly erodes."
-Kal Yeary

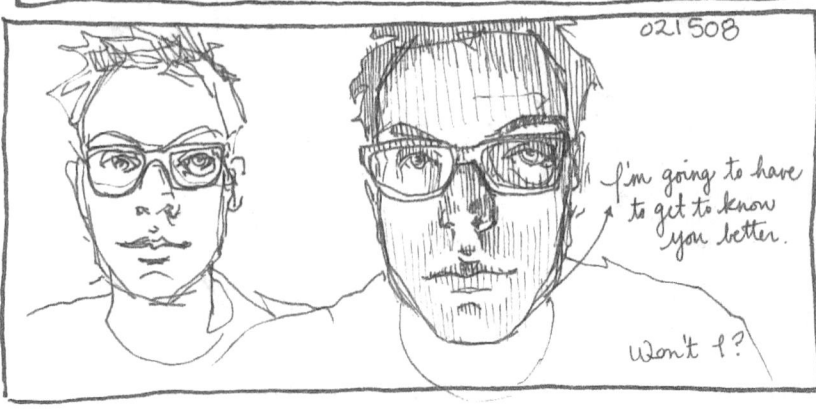

i'm going to have to get to know you better.

Won't I?

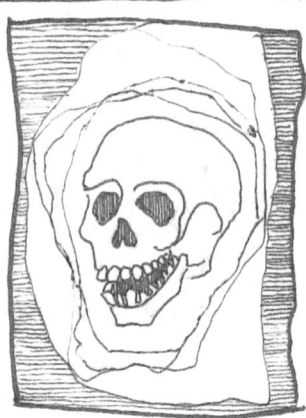

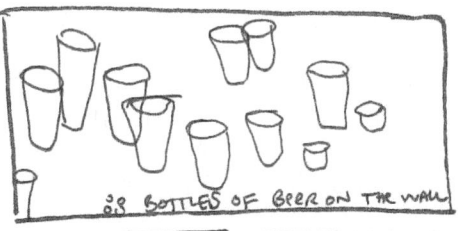

?? BOTTLES OF BEER ON THE WALL

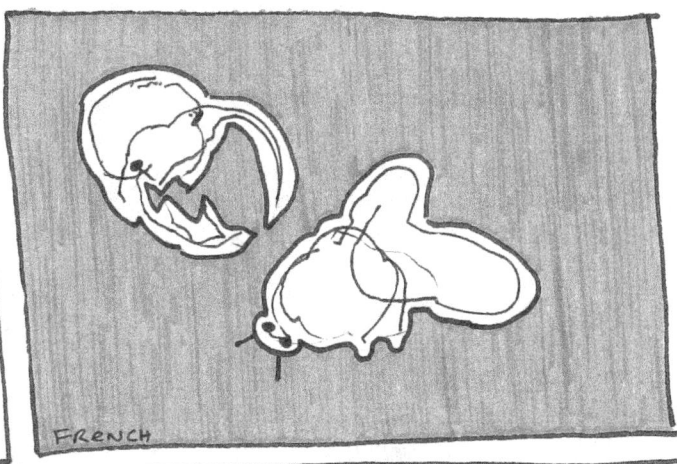

FRENCH

BUB WOO-EY

ay 13, 17
and oth
dopted
the gover
ment. Abc
WE NEED TO BE

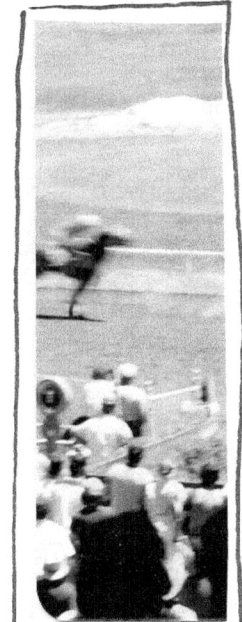

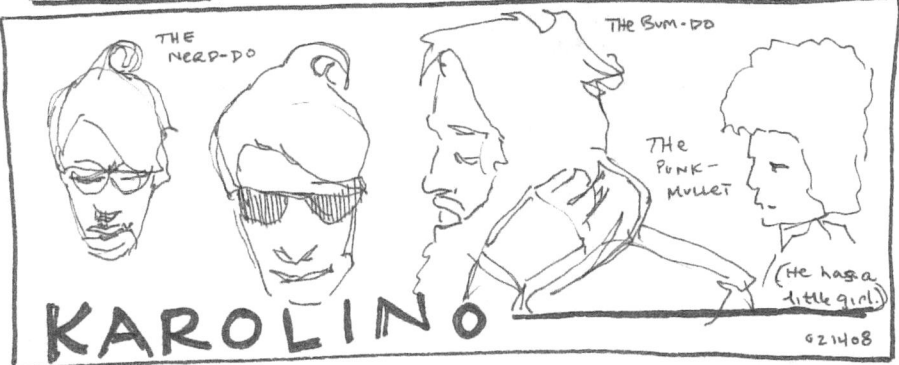

THE
NERD-DO

THE BUM-DO

THE
PUNK-
MULLET

(He has a
little girl.)

KAROLINO

021408

DATE PAIM

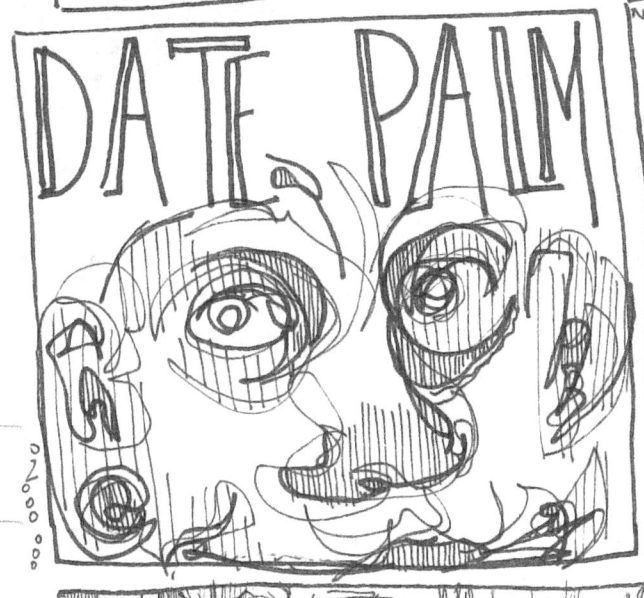

070,000,000

021308

NOT ME — GOD BLESS

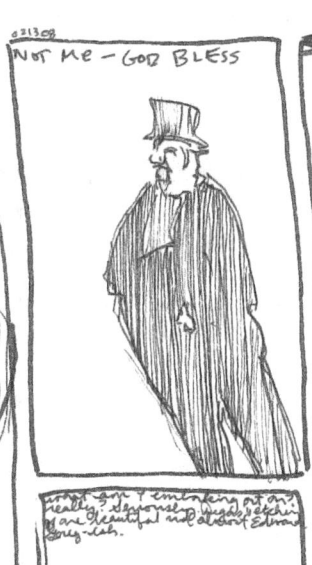

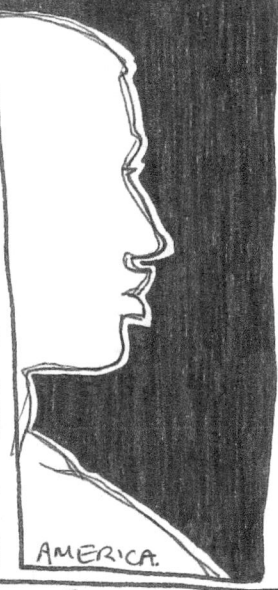

AMERICA.

TABASCO

BISCUIT
EAR

BISCUITS CAFE

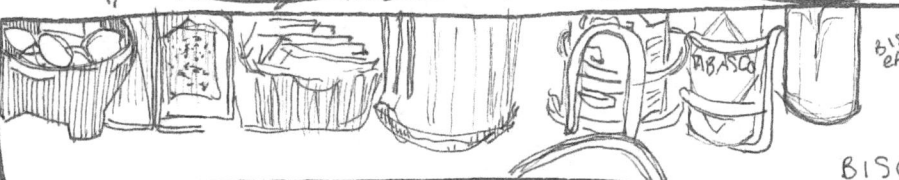

AMEN...

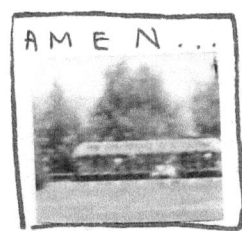

021408

FOR
BUCKETS

RP IS SHE STILL MARRIED
I'M SURPRISED IT LASTED...99

BLITZ
IN THE PEARL

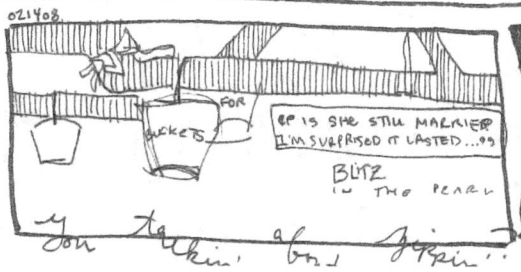

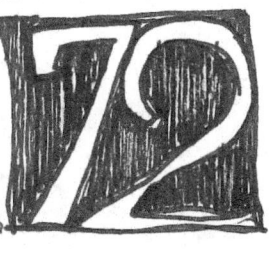

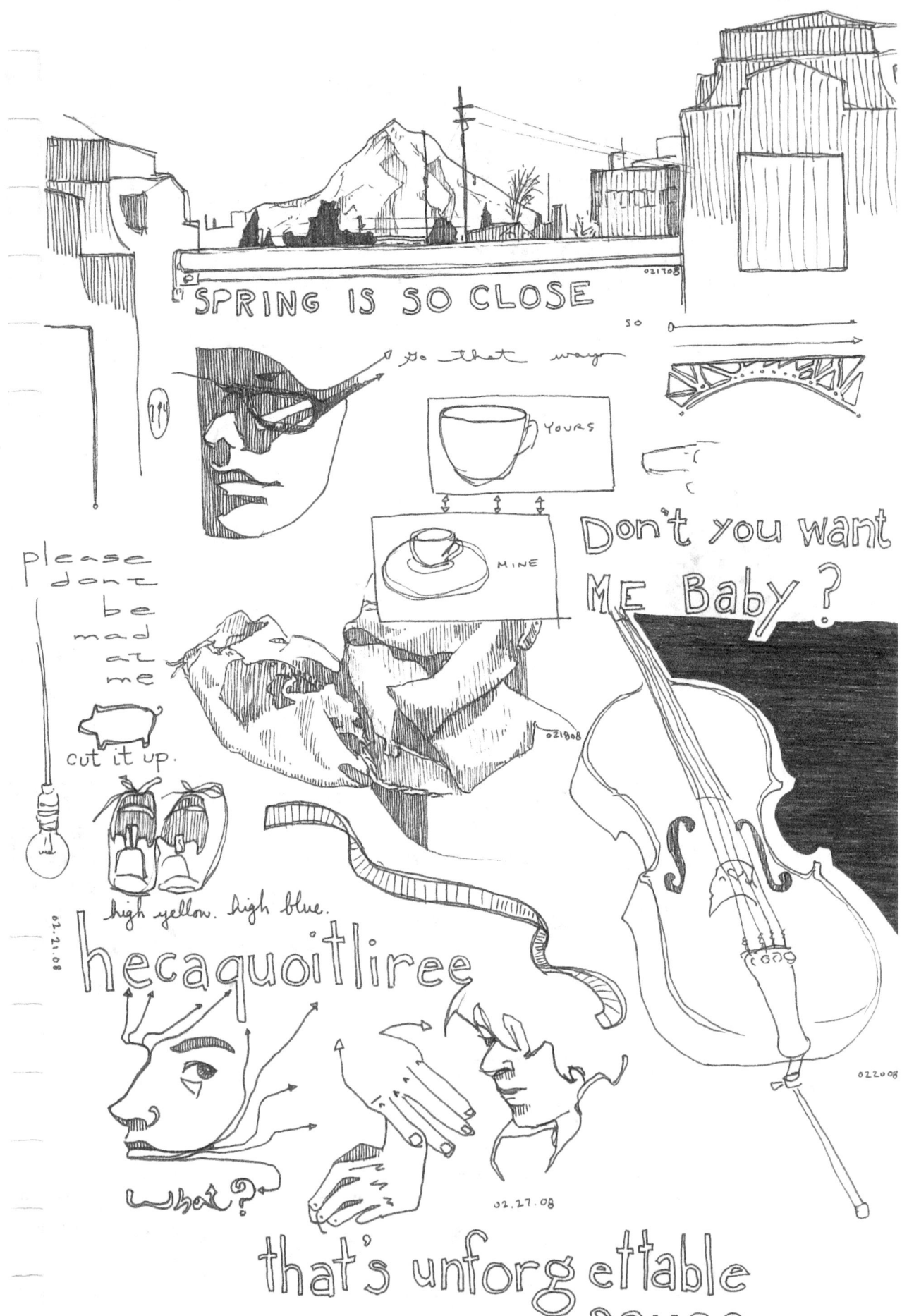

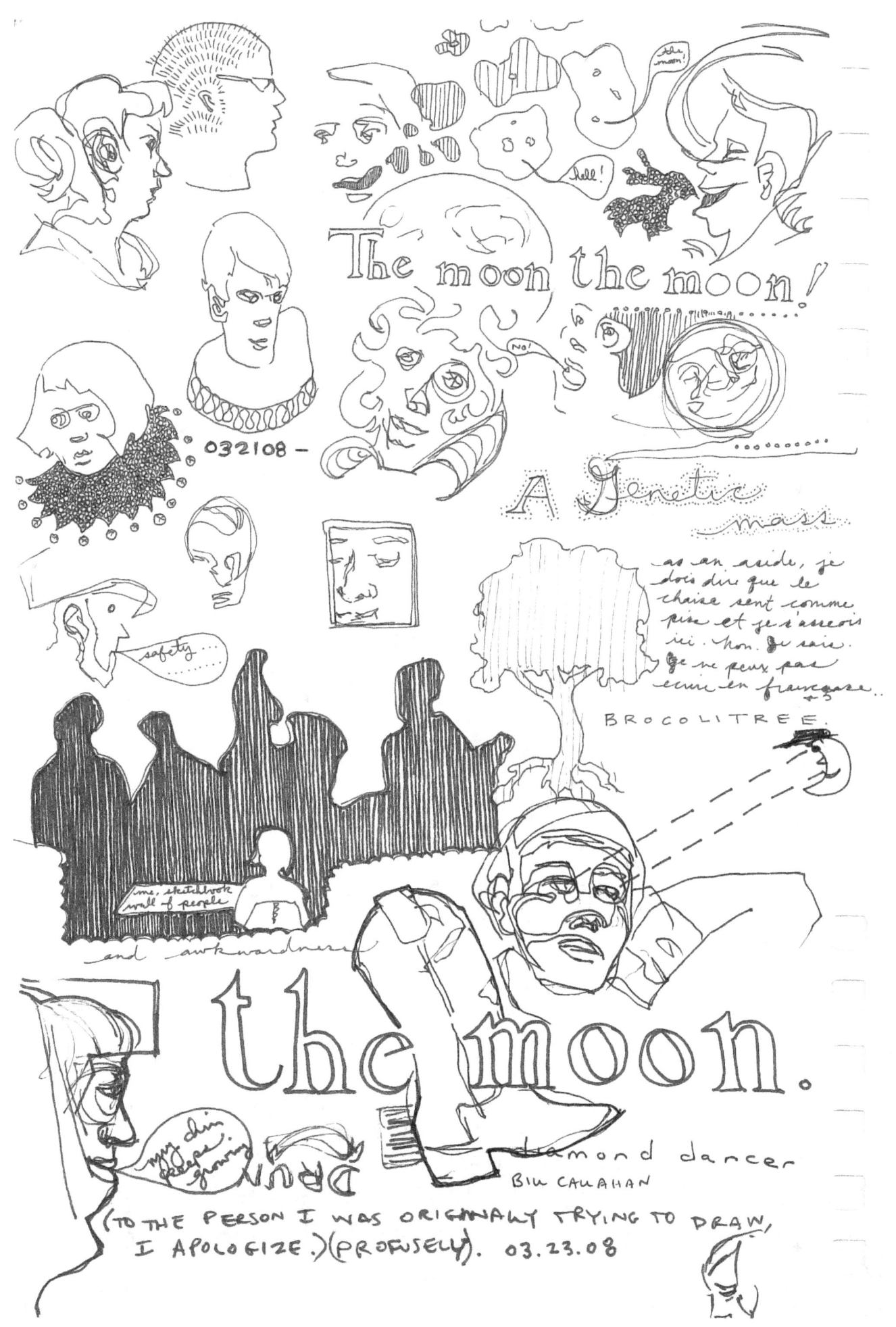

HAVE PATIENCE.
IT WILL BENEFIT YOU.

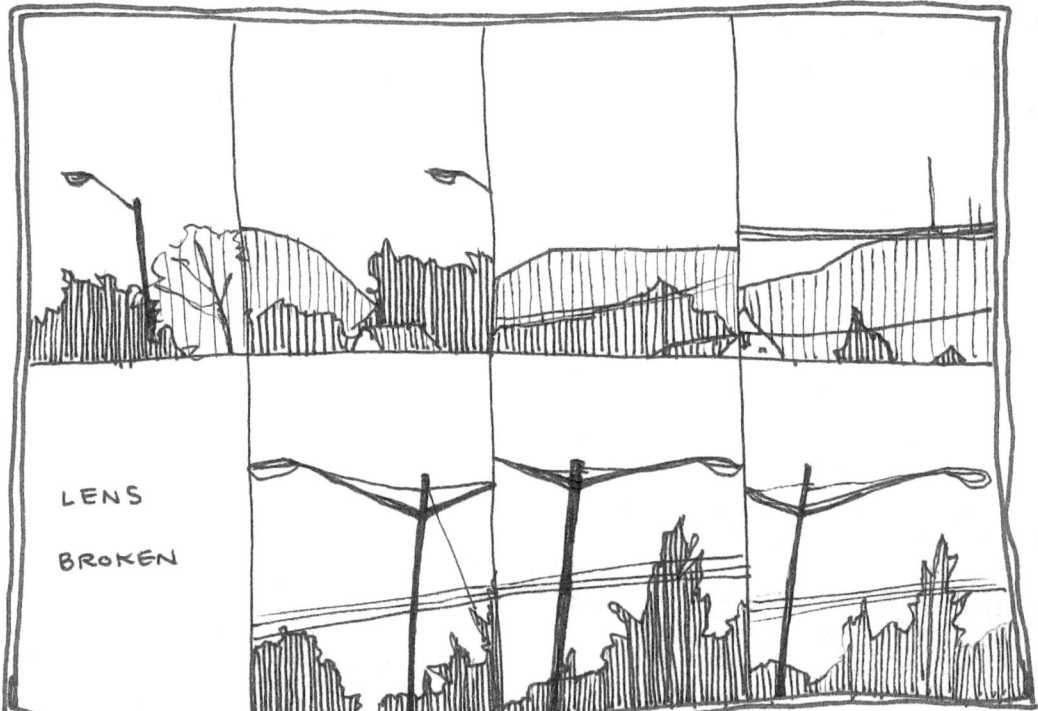

LENS

BROKEN

YOUR HOME IS A PLEASANT PLACE
FROM WHICH YOU DRAW HAPPINESS

YOU WILL LIVE TO A RIPE OLD
AGE; HAPPY IN LOVE AND
RESPECT OF MANY CHILDREN.

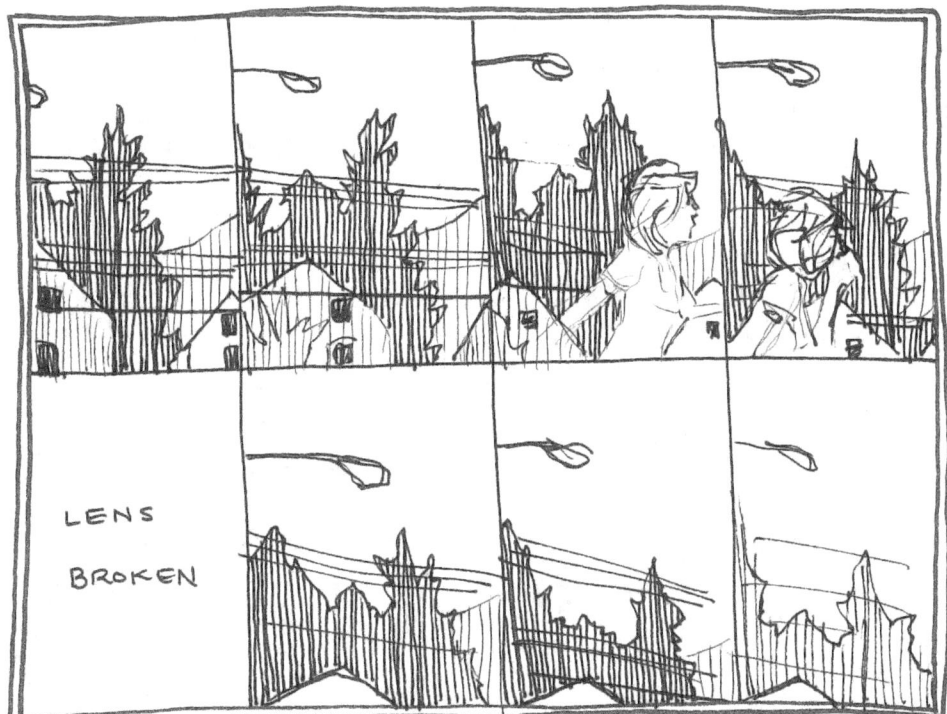

LENS

BROKEN

A PAST ACQUAINTANCE WILL
SOON RE-ENTER YOUR LIFE.

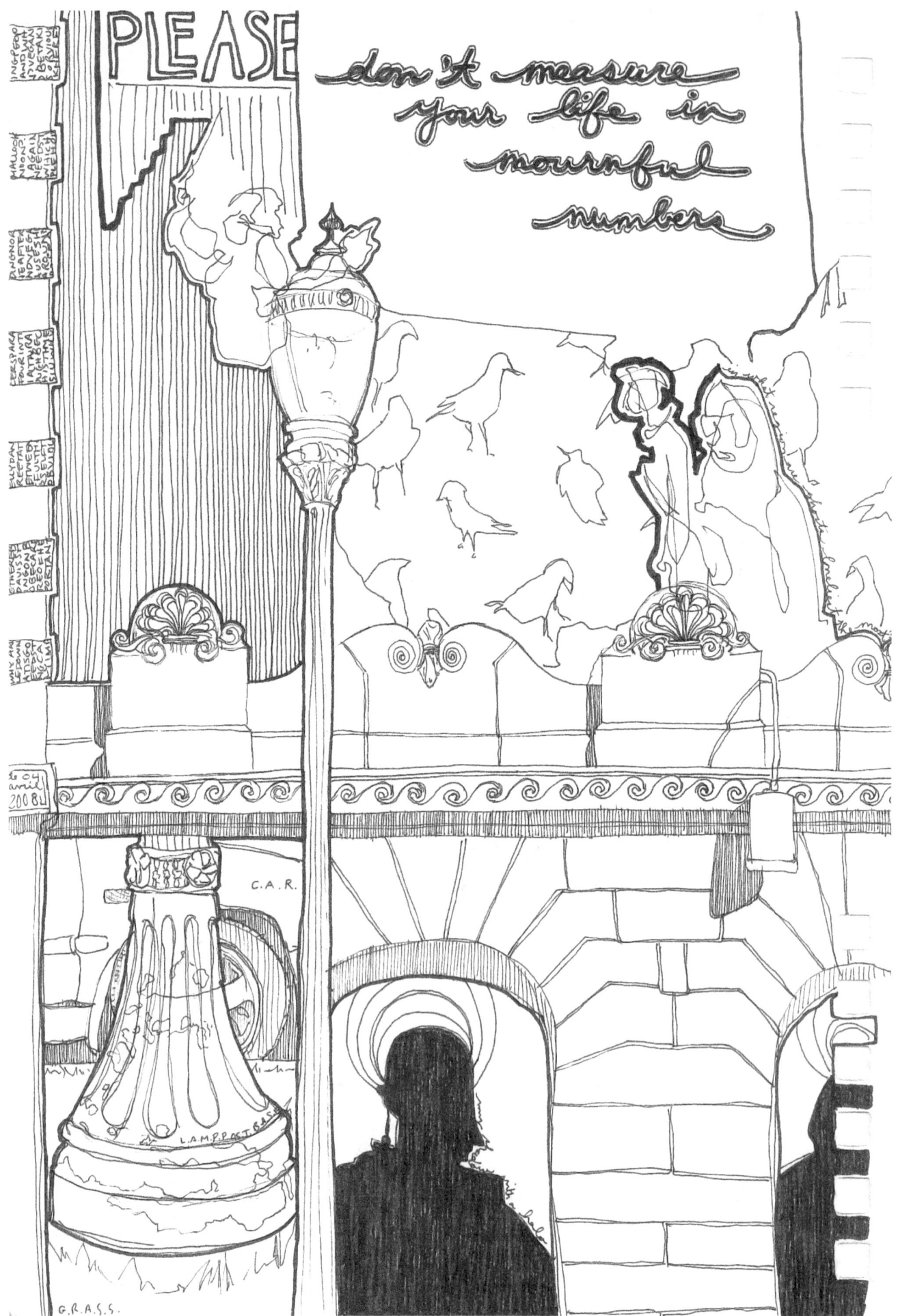

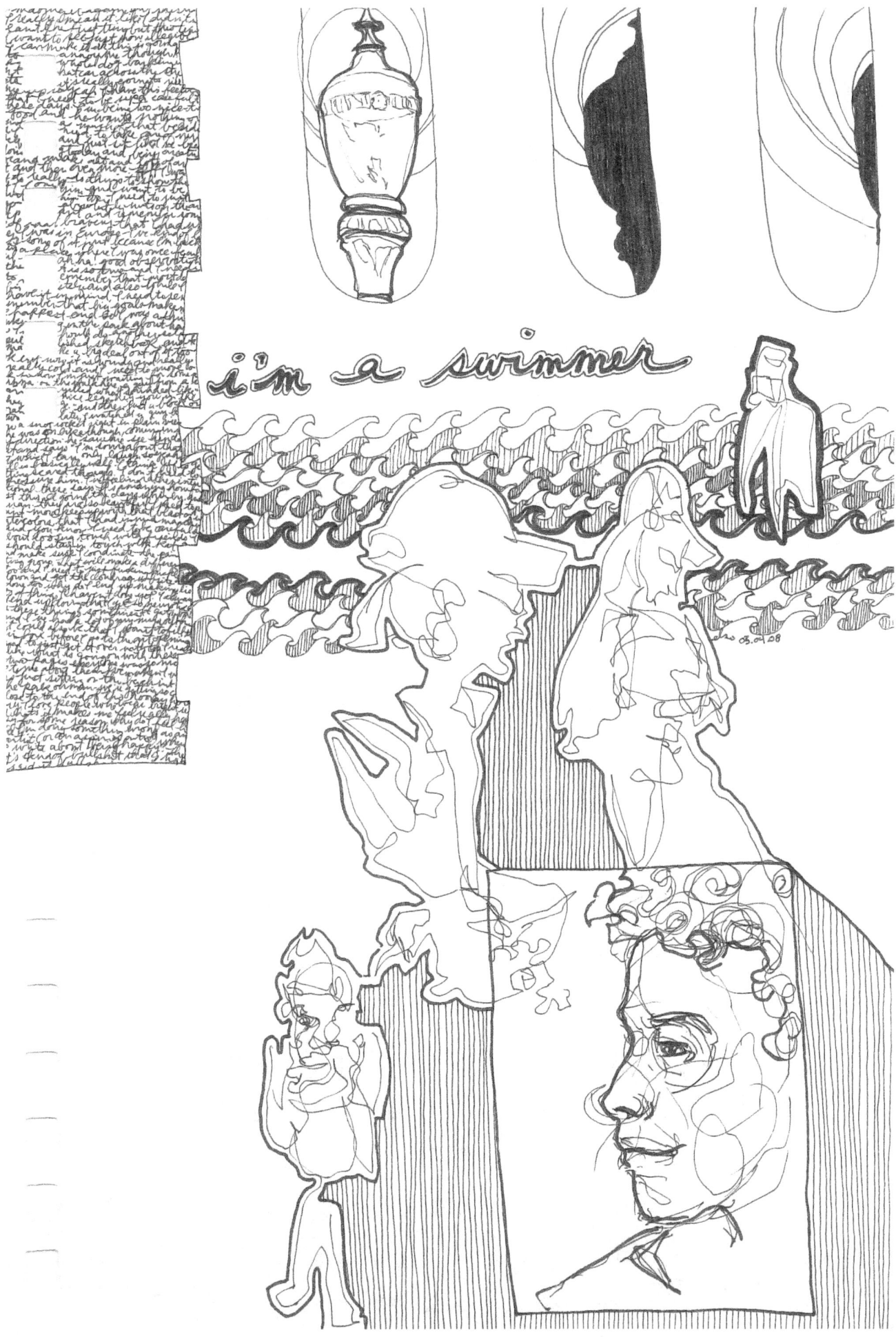

i'm a swimmer

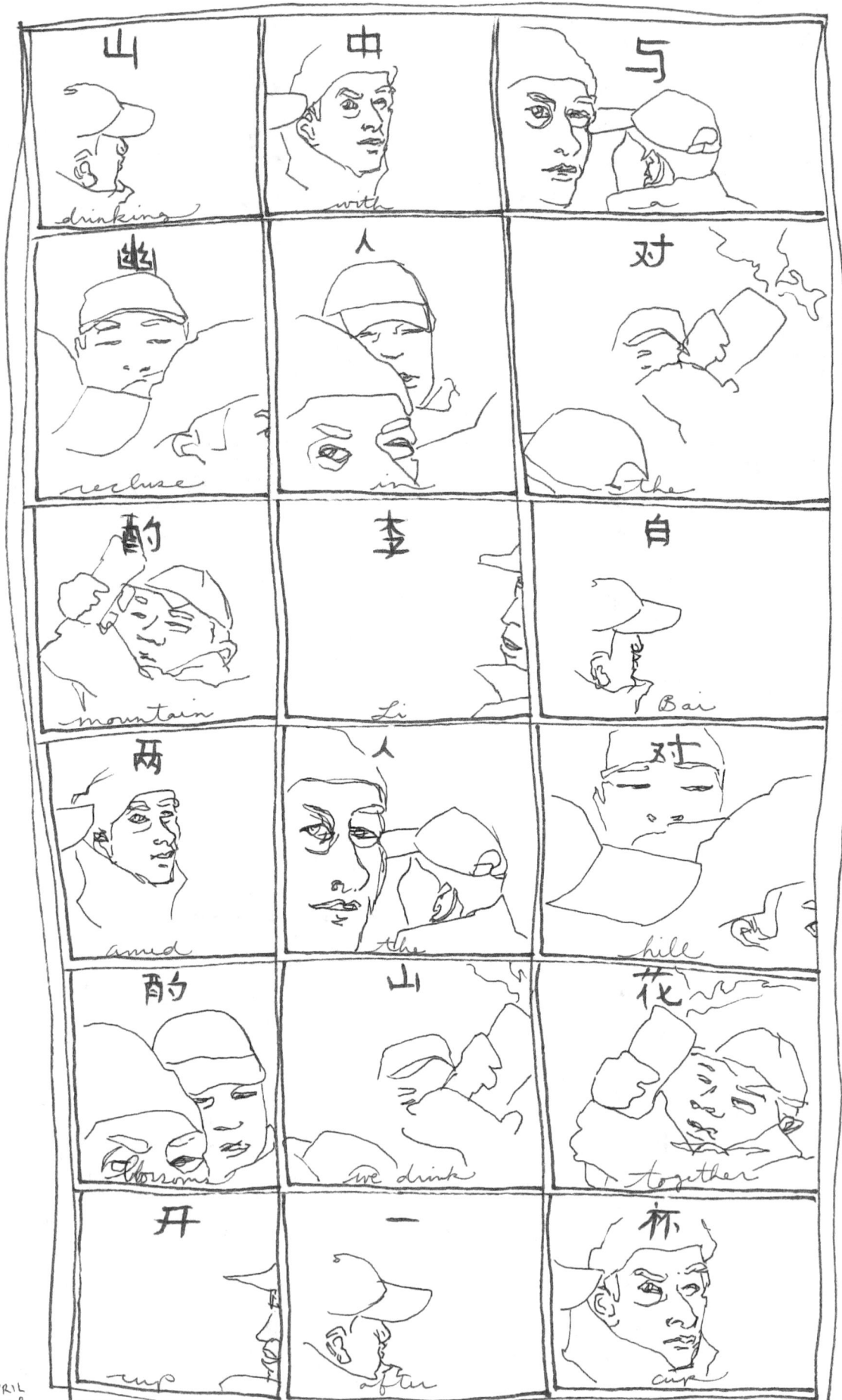

山　drinking
中　with
与
幽　recluse
人　in
对　the
酌　mountain
李　Li
白　Bai
两　amid
人　the
对　hill
酌　blossoms
山　we drink
花　together
开　cup
一　after
杯　cup

APRIL
2008

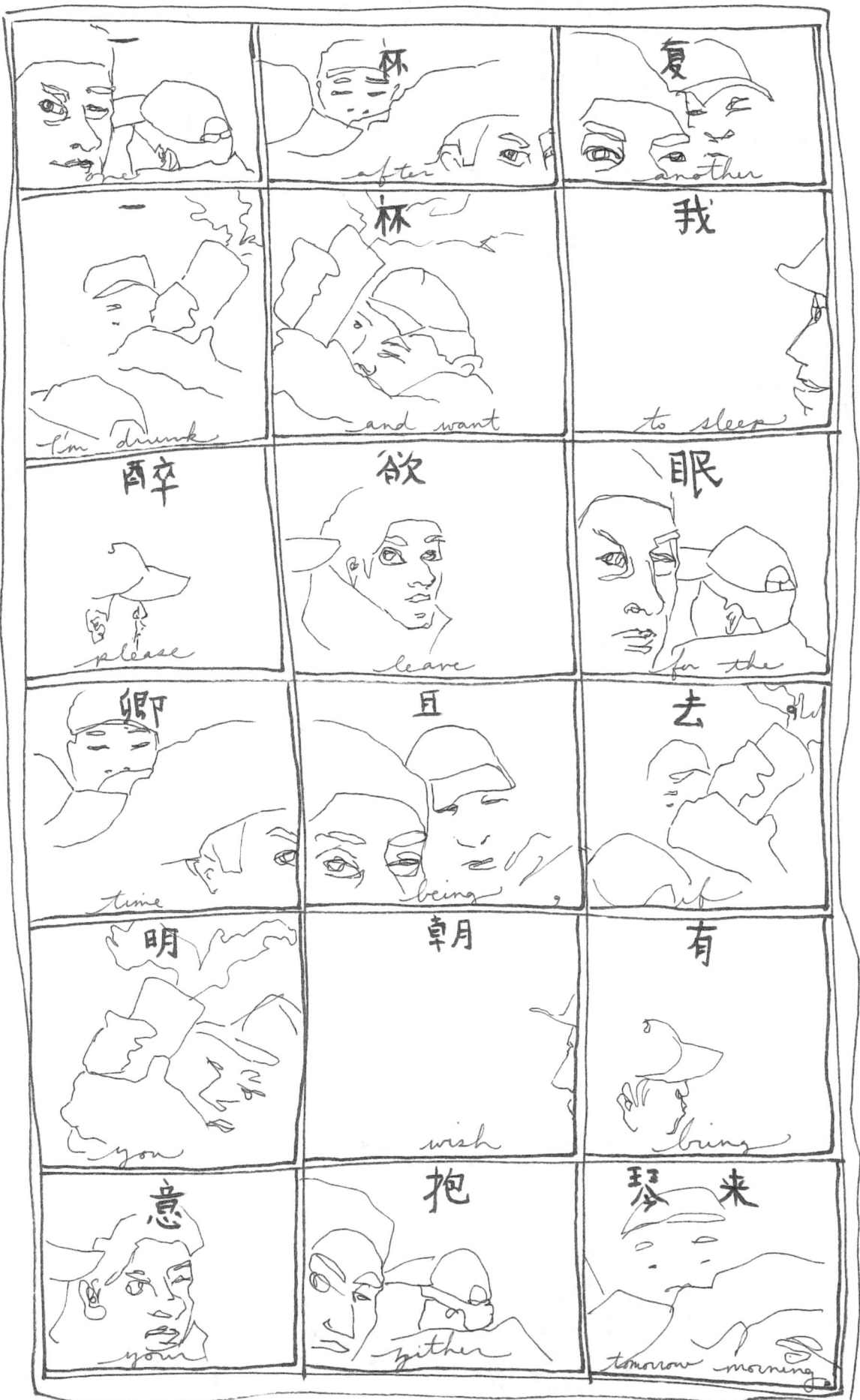

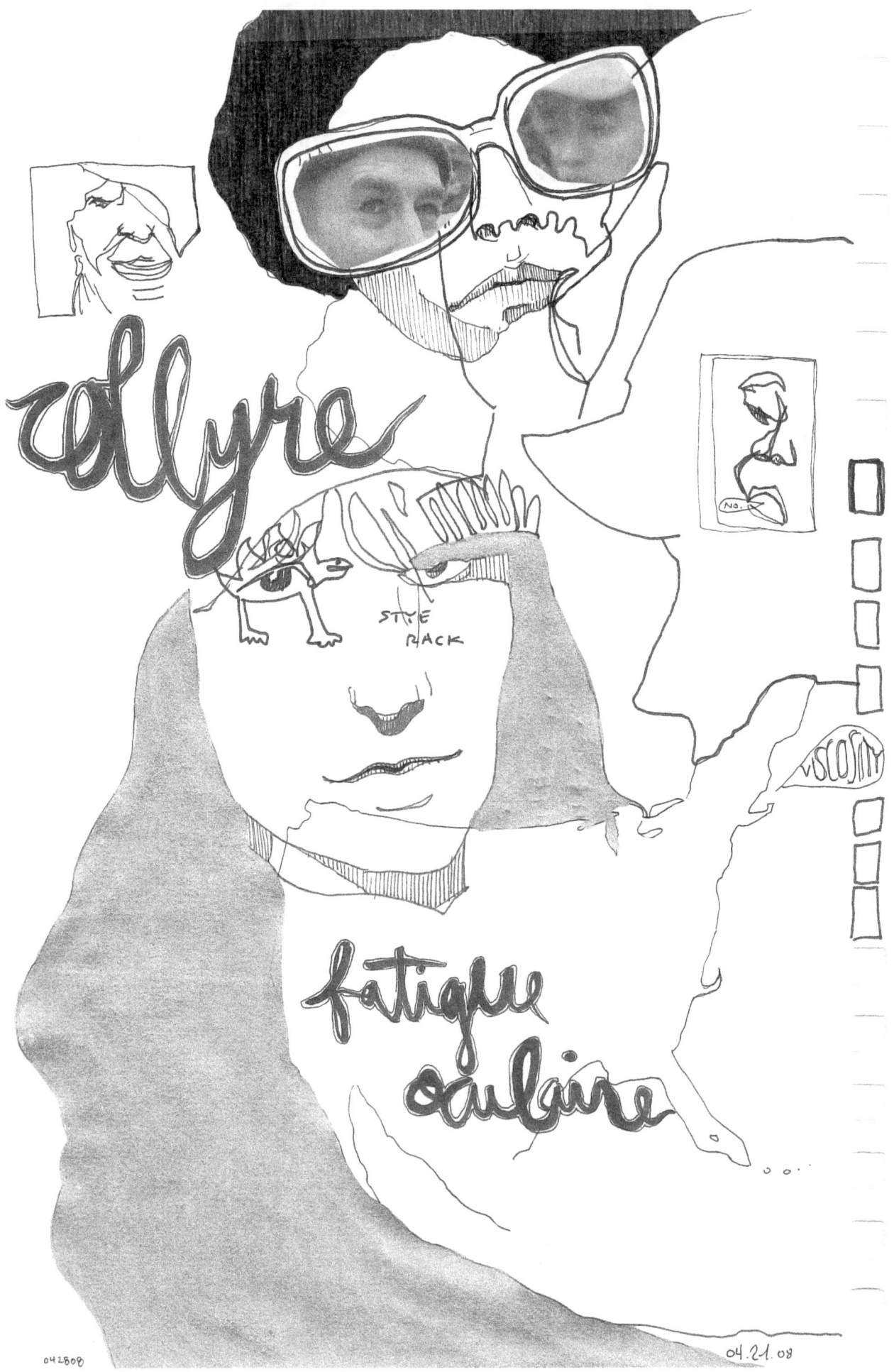

délyre

STYLE
RACK

VISCOSITY

NO.

fatigue
oculaire

042808

04.21.08

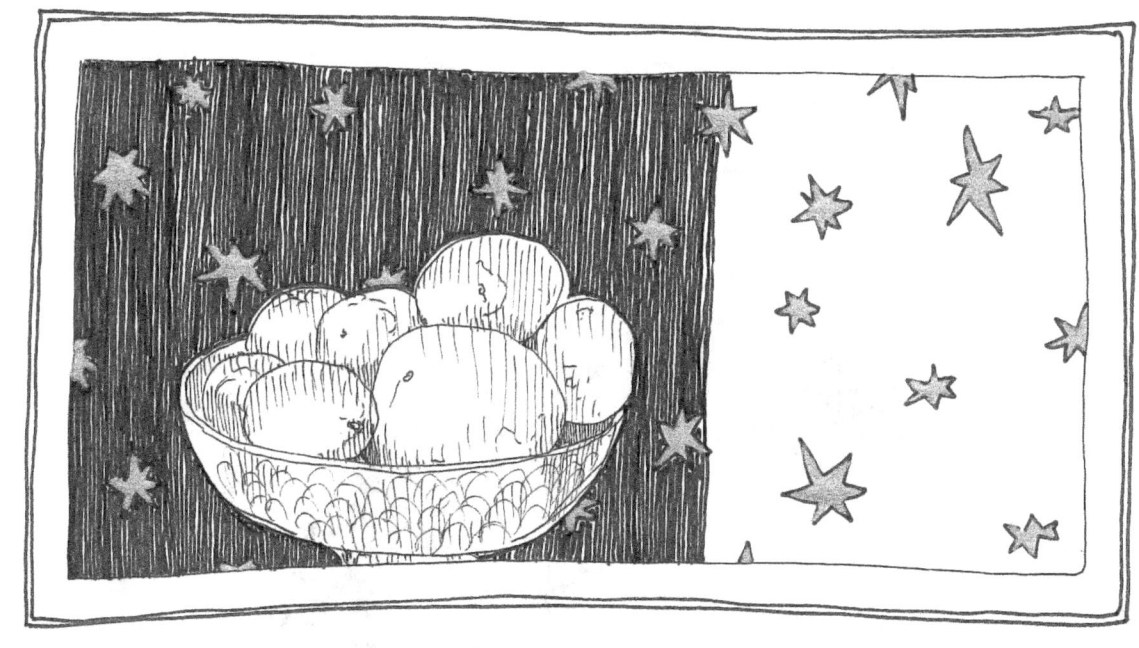

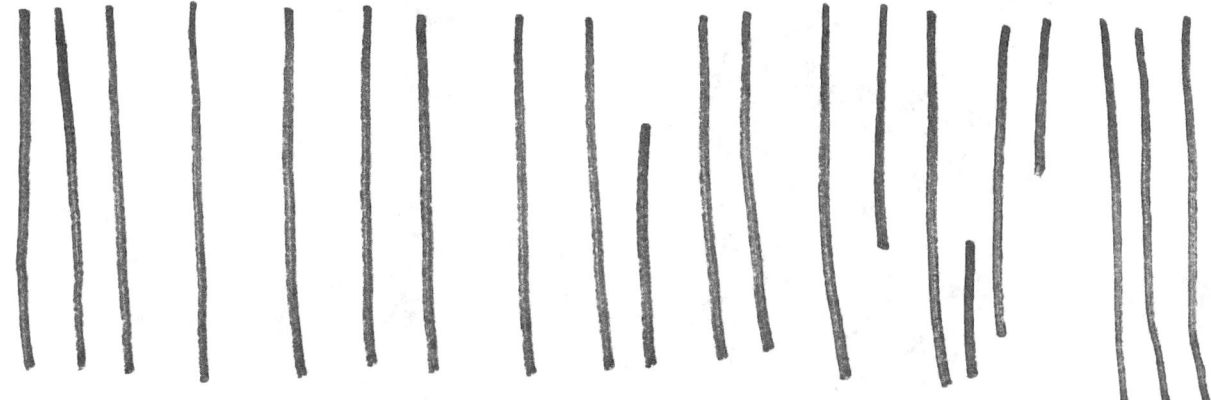

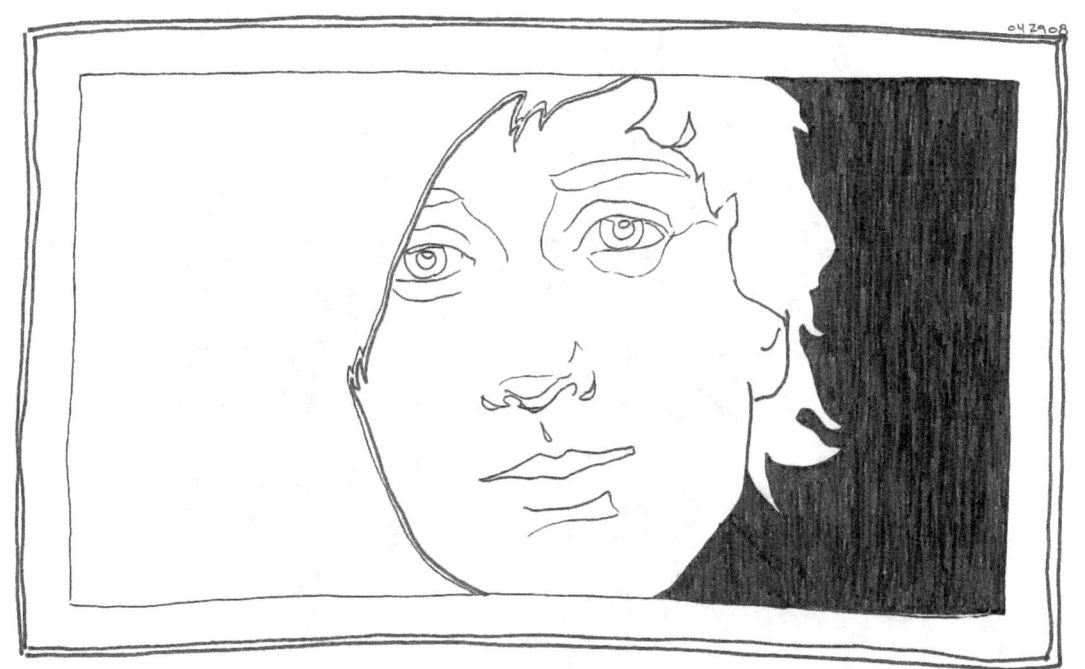

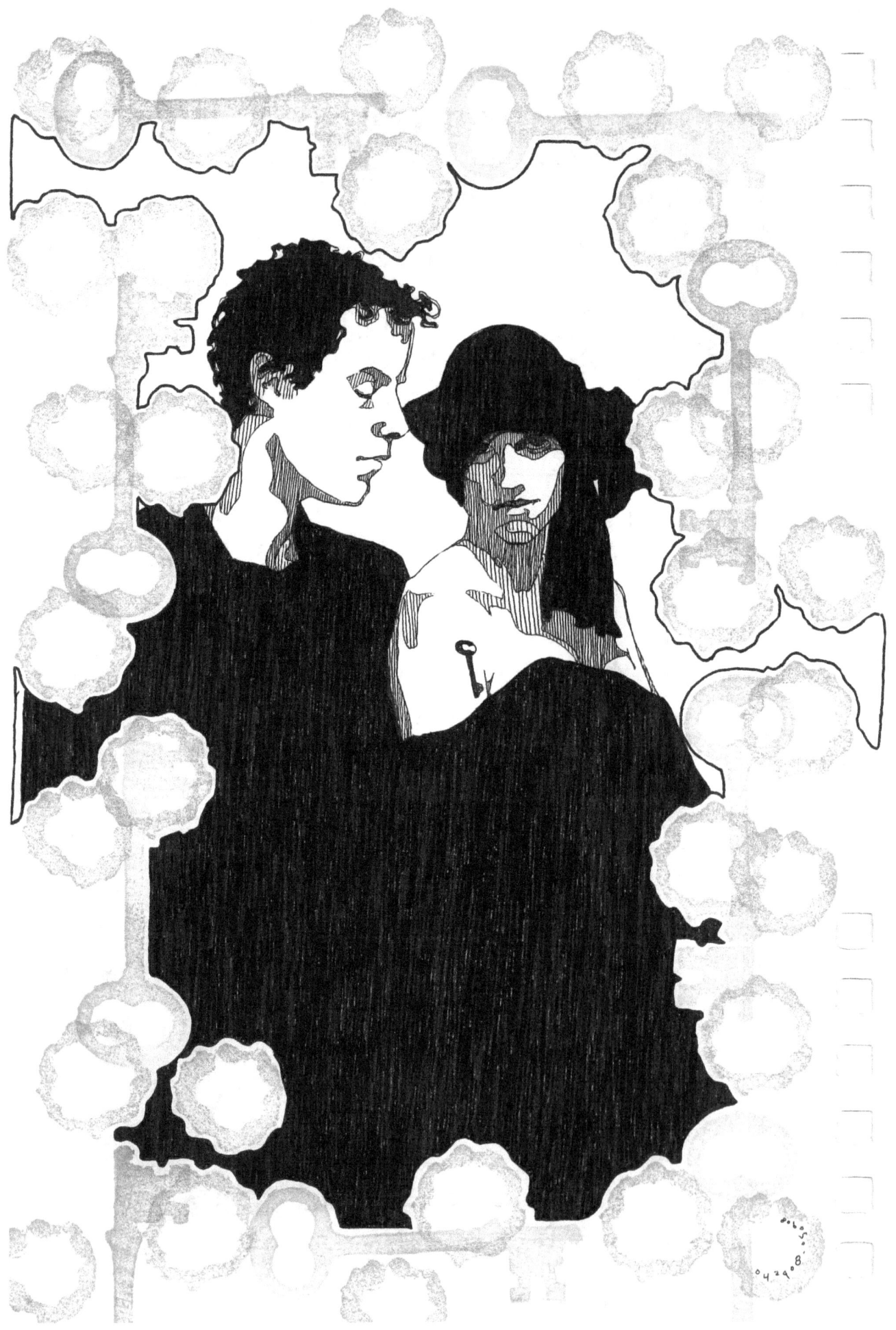

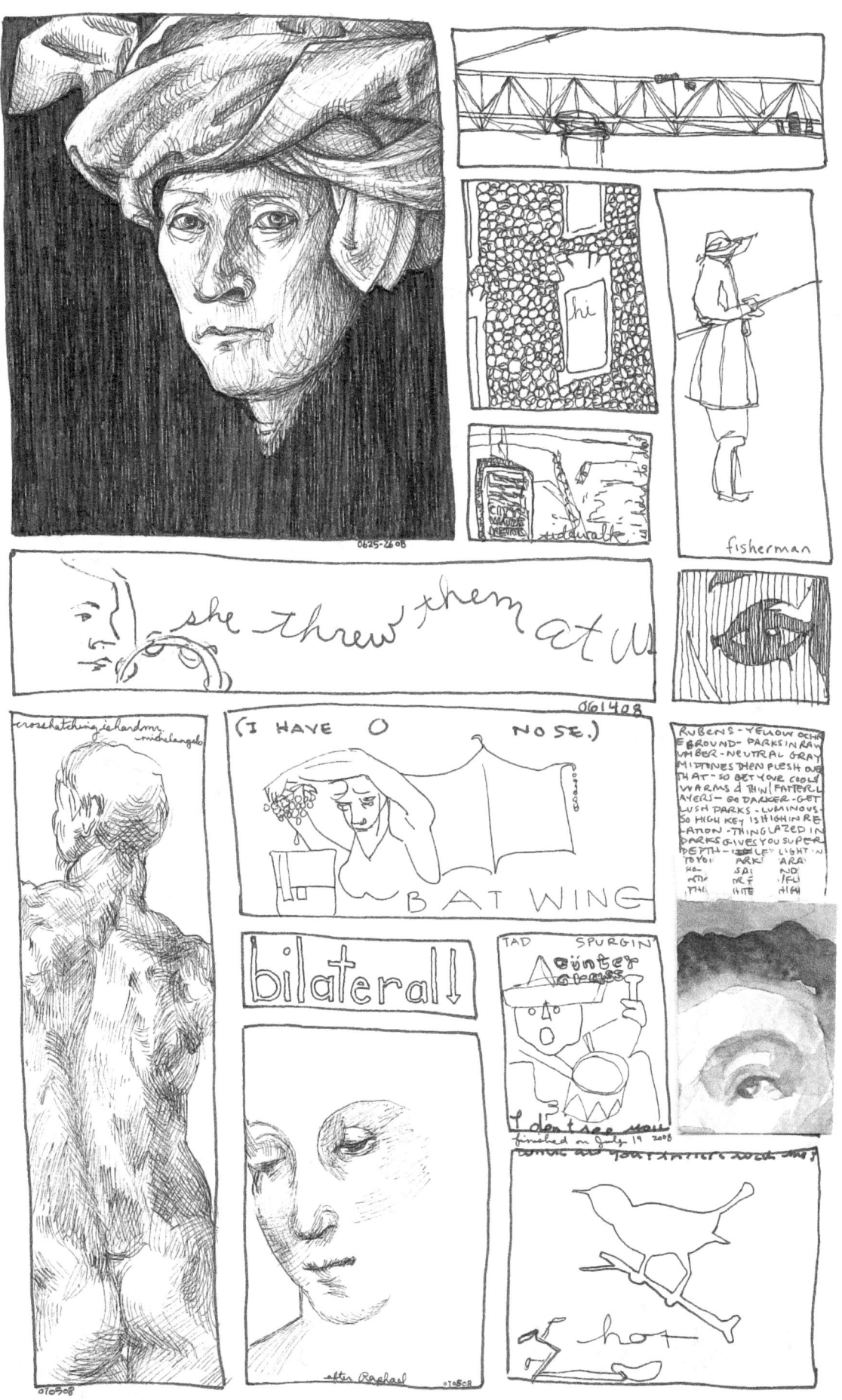

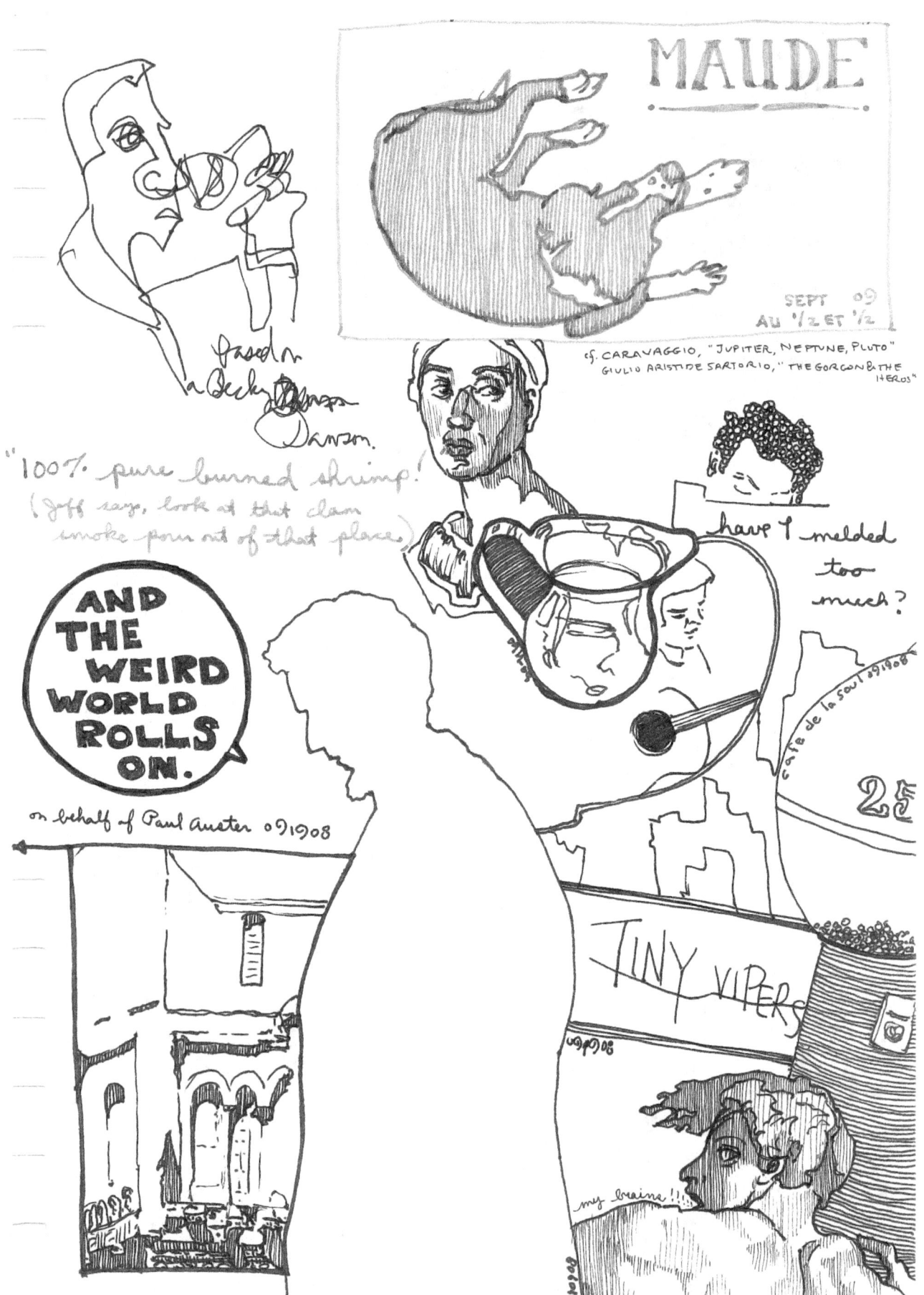

ON THE INSIDE POINT
OF A QUESTION THAT YOU BROUGHT ME TO
IN THE HALF-HOUSE
THAT YOUR DADDY BUILT THAT SWEAR TO KEEP
WITH THE TRAINS WHISTLIN' BY
ECHOES ON THE HILLSIDE

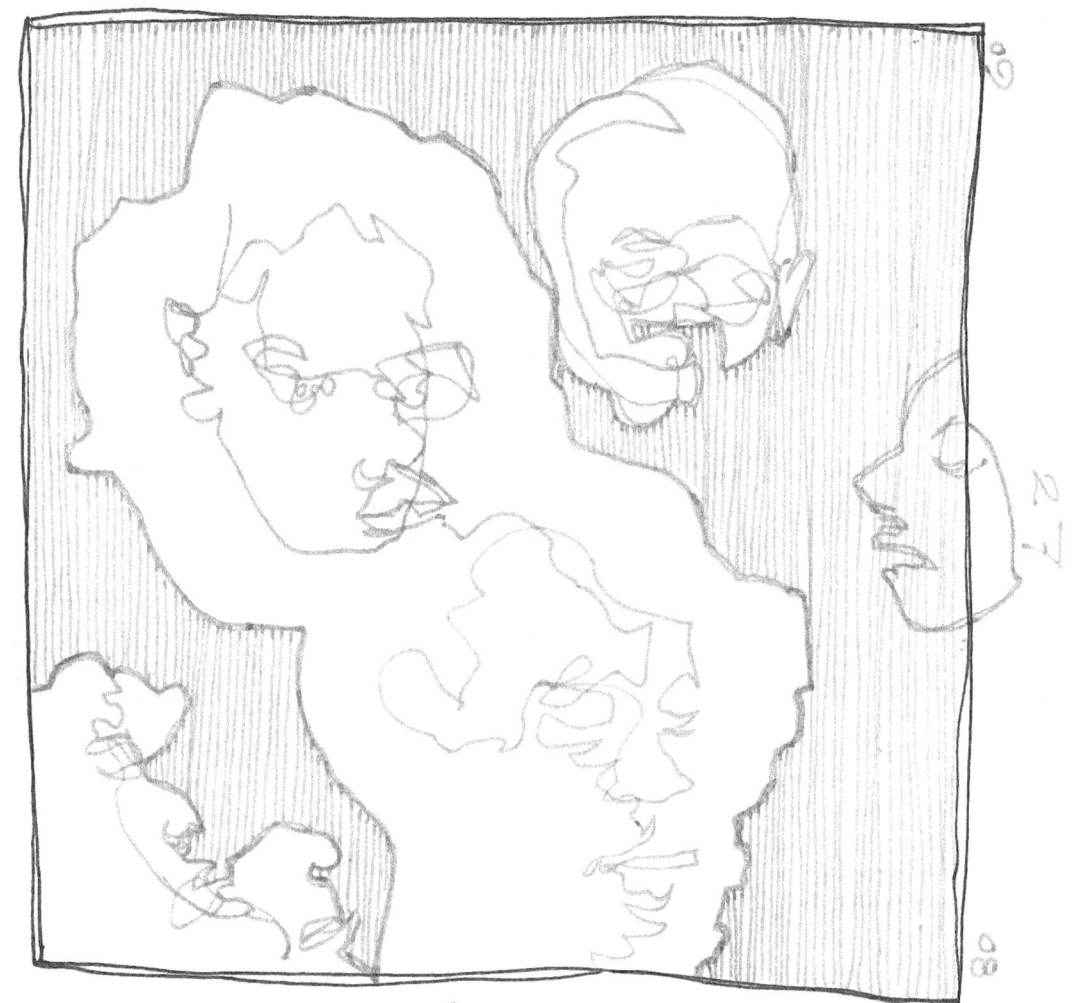

Those who feel eternity
are above all fear.
R.M.R.

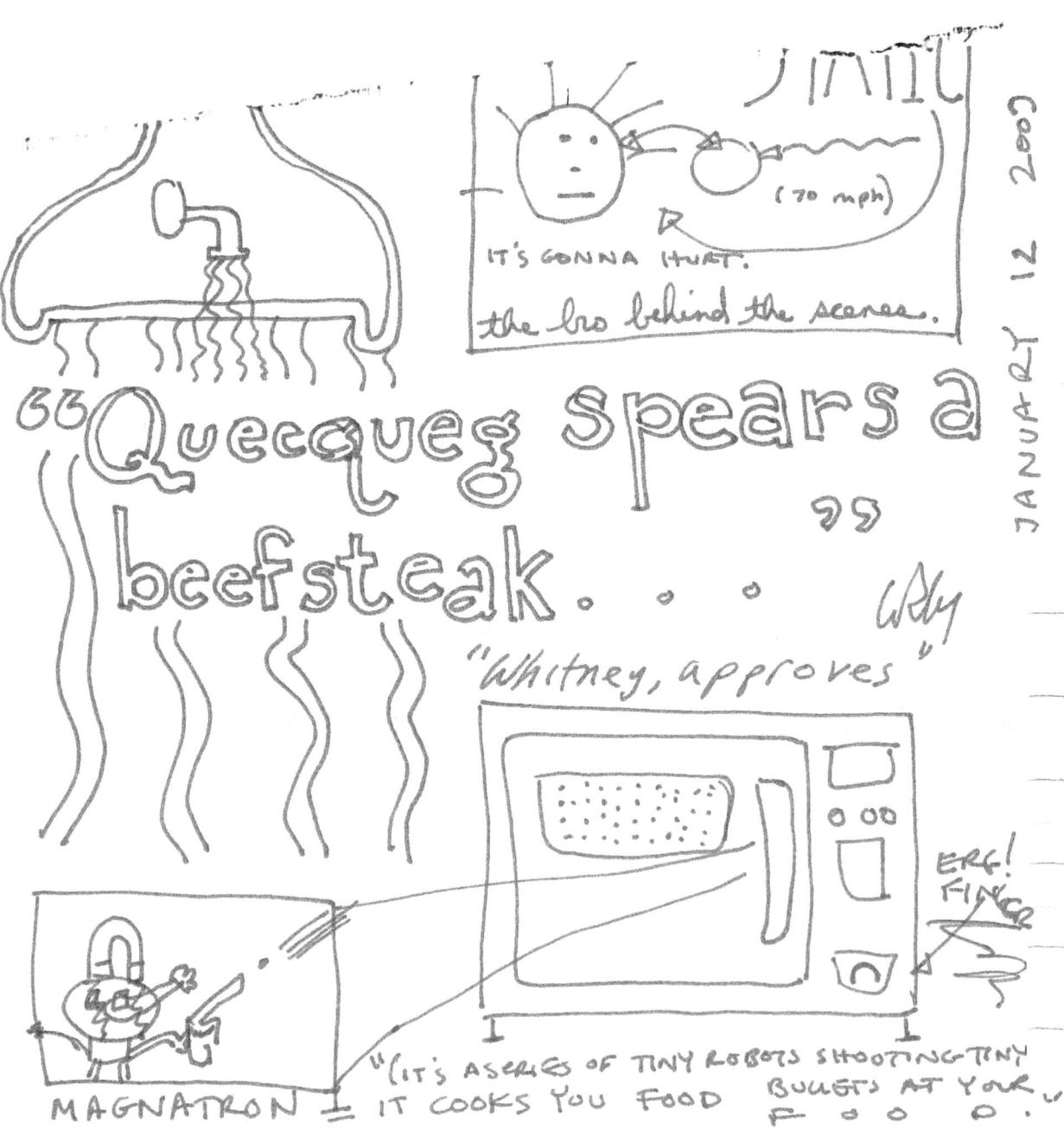

IT'S GONNA HURT.

(70 mph)

the bro behind the scenes.

"Quecqueg spears a beefsteak. . . . ˚   ˚

Wly

"Whitney, approves"

ERG!
FINGER

MAGNATRON = IT COOKS YOU FOOD "(IT'S A SERIES OF TINY ROBOTS SHOOTING TINY BULLETS AT YOUR F O O D.

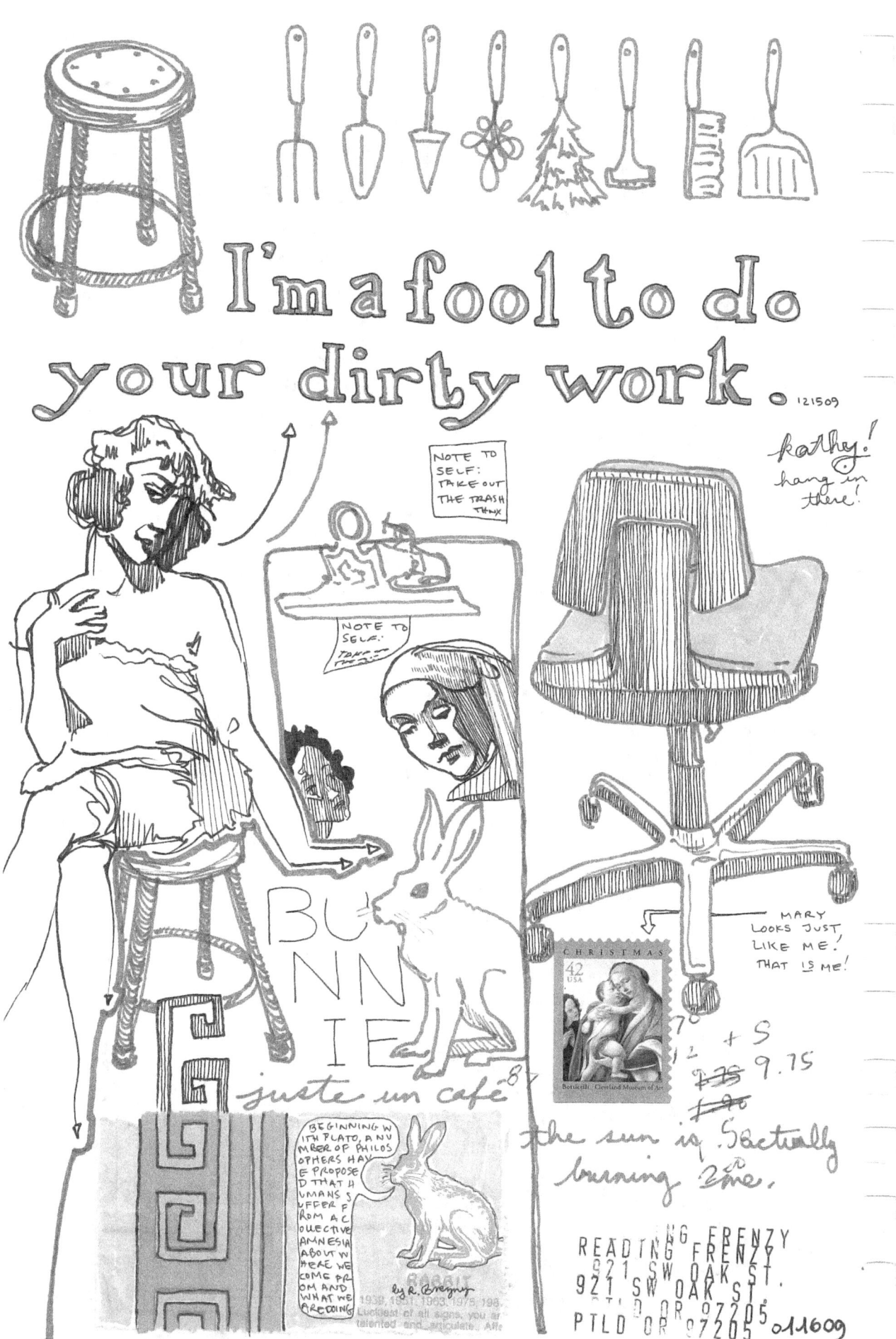

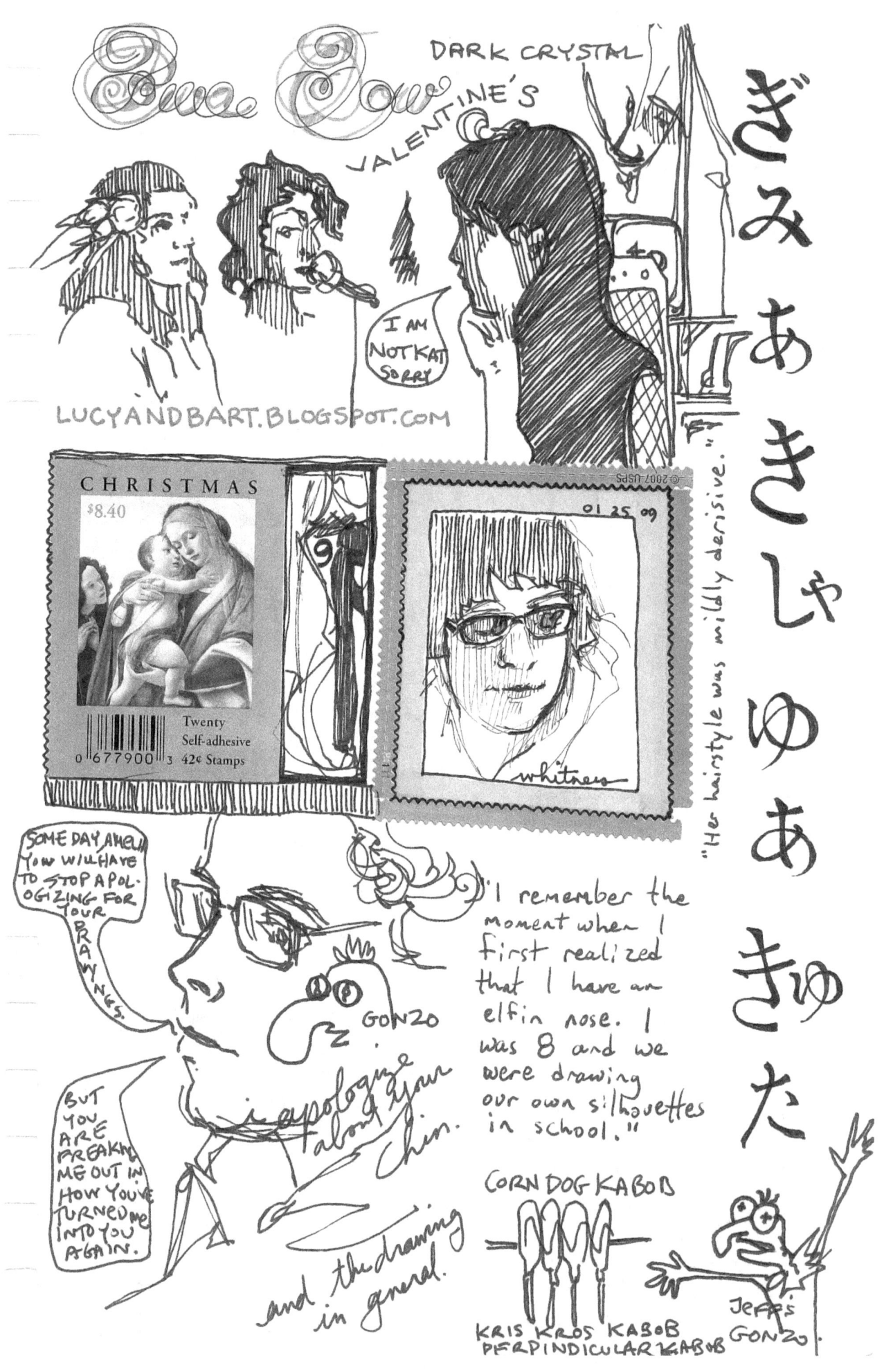

STARTED 012509

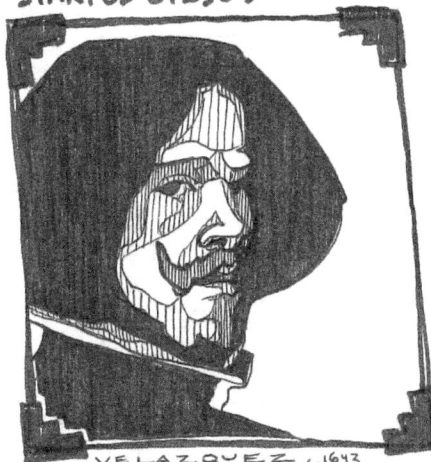

VELAZQUEZ c.1643

ENDED 032009

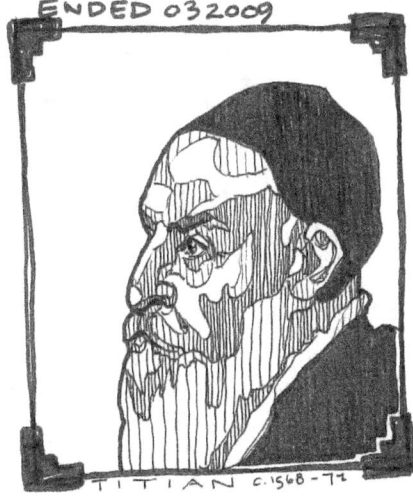

TITIAN c.1568-71

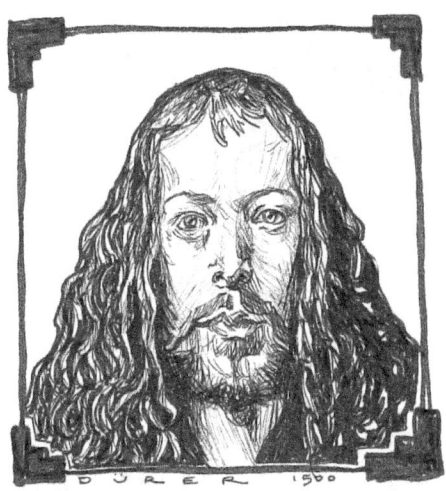

DÜRER 1500

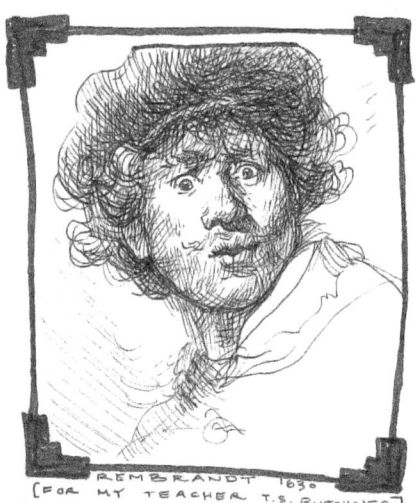

REMBRANDT 1630
(FOR MY TEACHER T.S. BUECHNER)

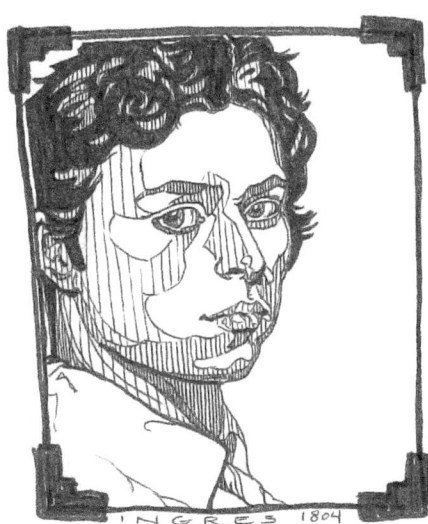

INGRES 1804

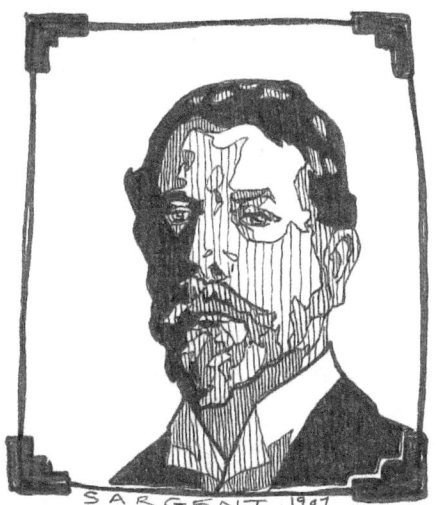

SARGENT 1907

SOMEBODY SMELLS
WONDERFUL.

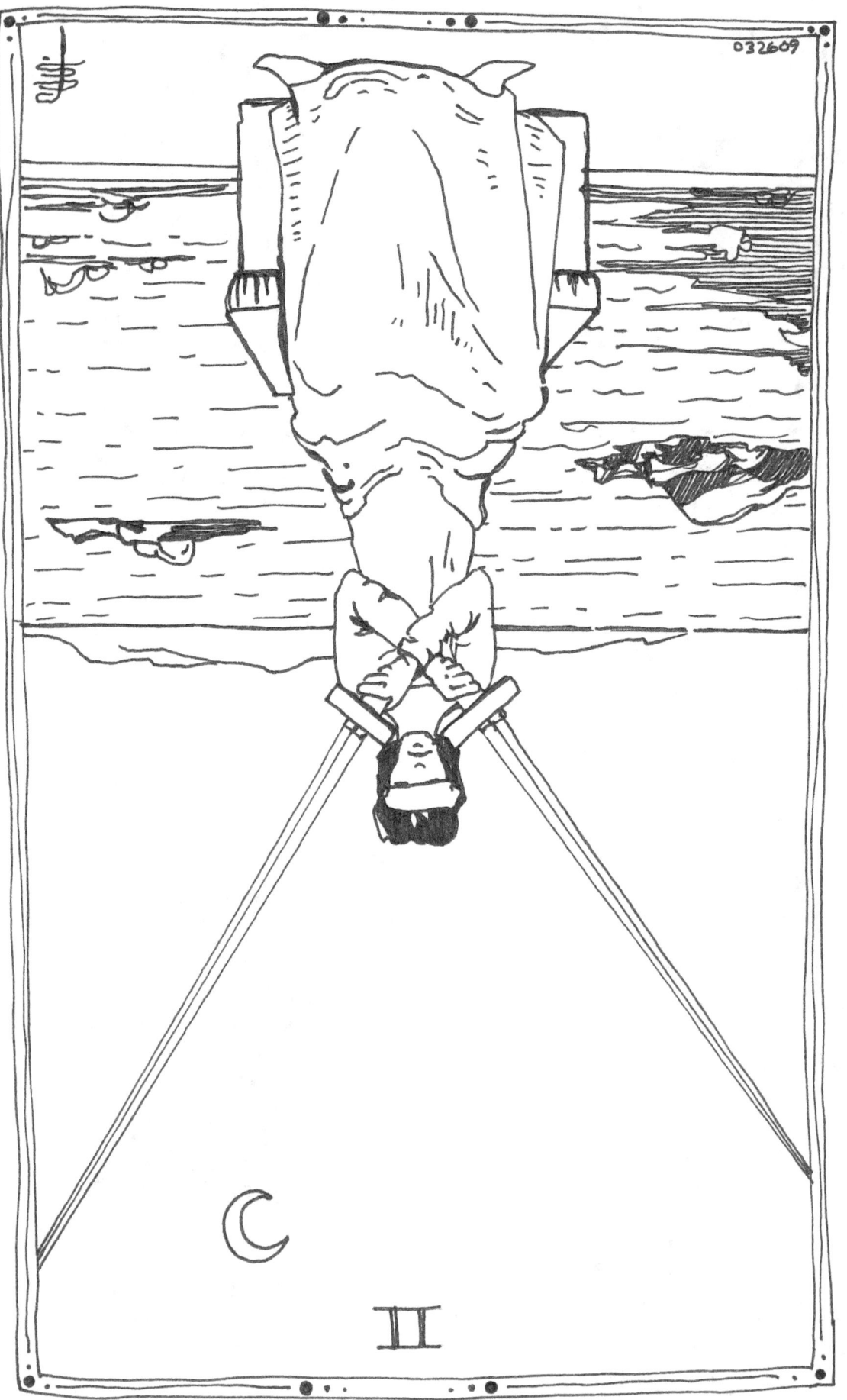

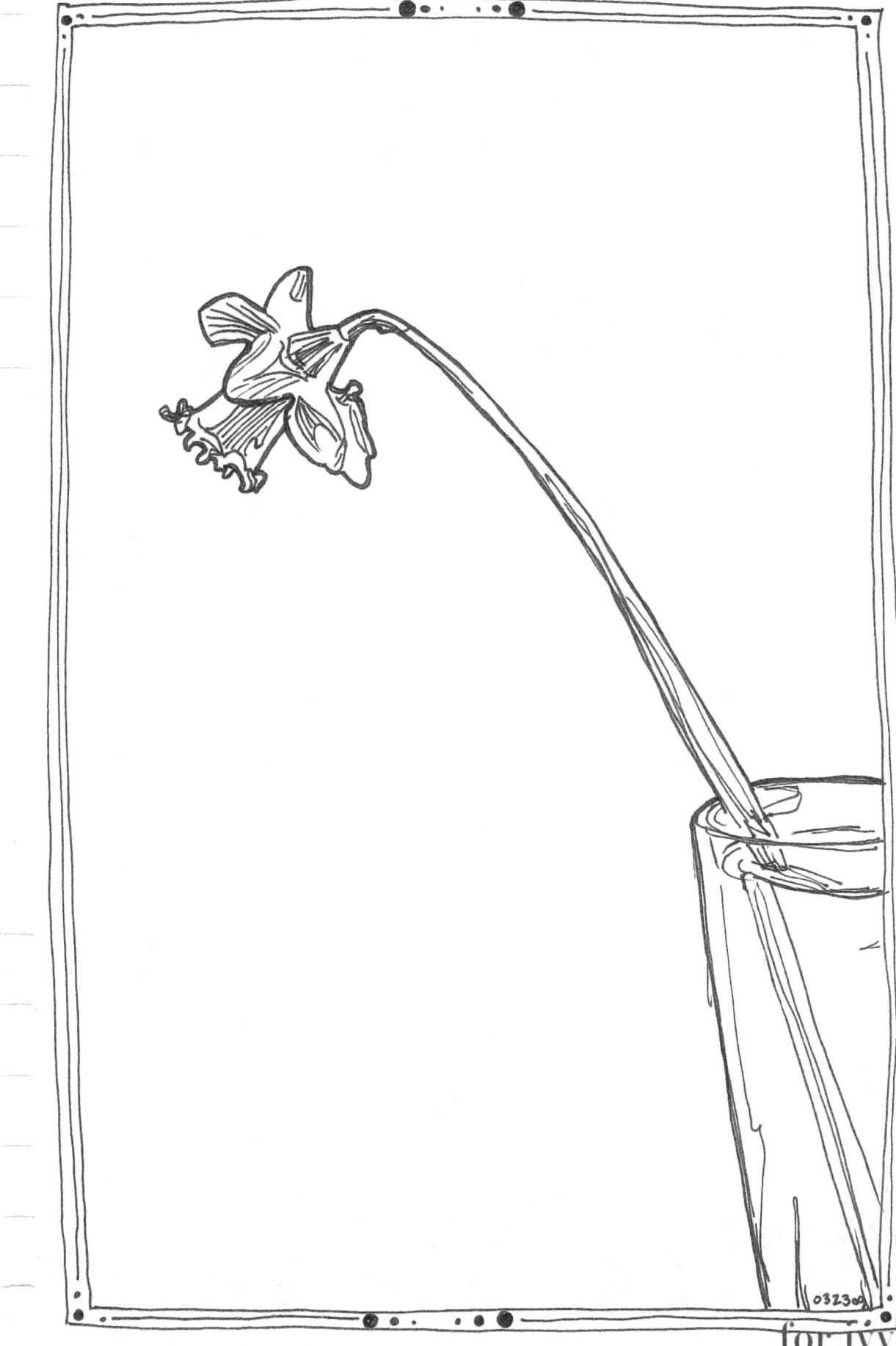

032300

for jvy

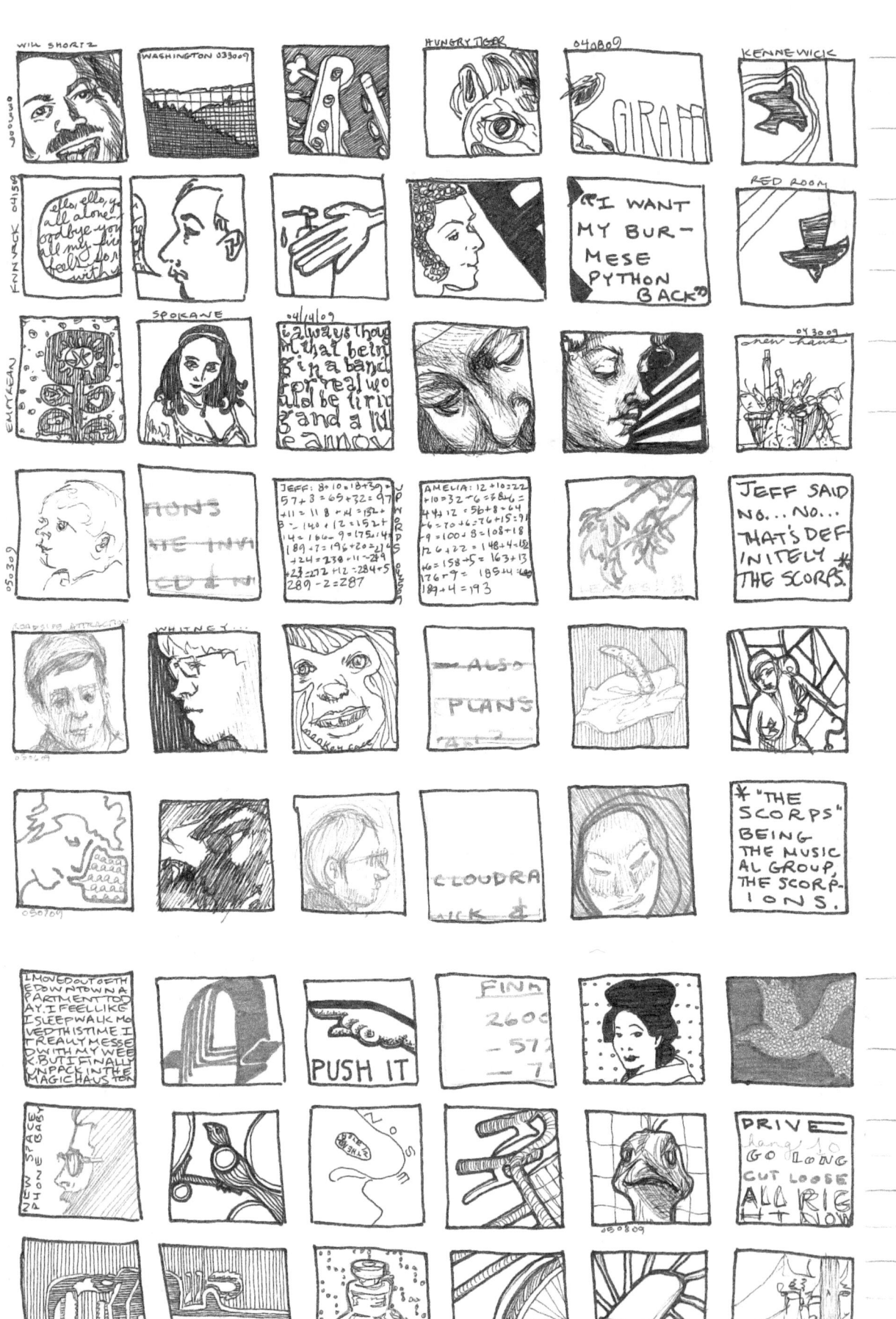

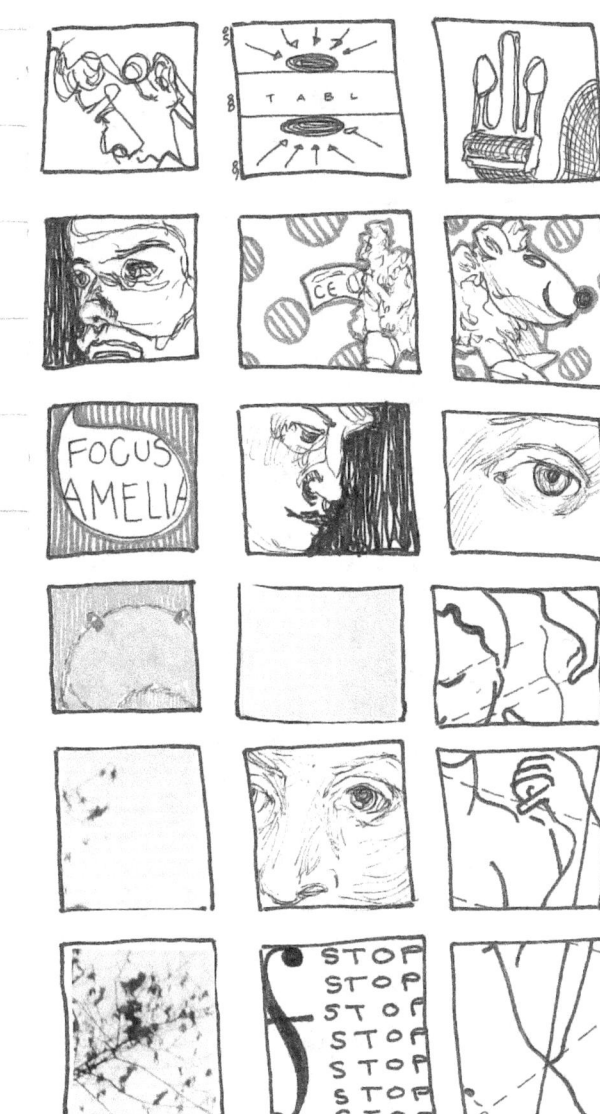

Seul l'Indépendant est le caractère qui donne toujours satisfaction a vos clients.

19

THE PARTITIVE ARTICLE (Cont.)

e partitive thought is also expressed by de w
article when a partitive noun in the plural i
led by an adjective:
'ai de vrais amis qui me donnent de bons cons
ave real friends who give me good advice.

T: the above rule does not apply when the adj
become associated with the noun so as to fo
d of compound name expressing a single idea.
e sont des jeunes gens qui disent des bons moi
n mangeant des petits pains et des petits pois.
re youth telling jokes while eating rolls and pe
here is also a tendency, in popular language, t
ne article before a partitive noun in the singula

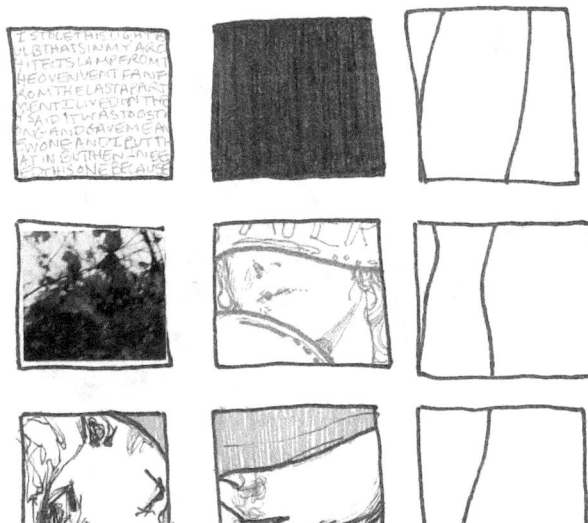

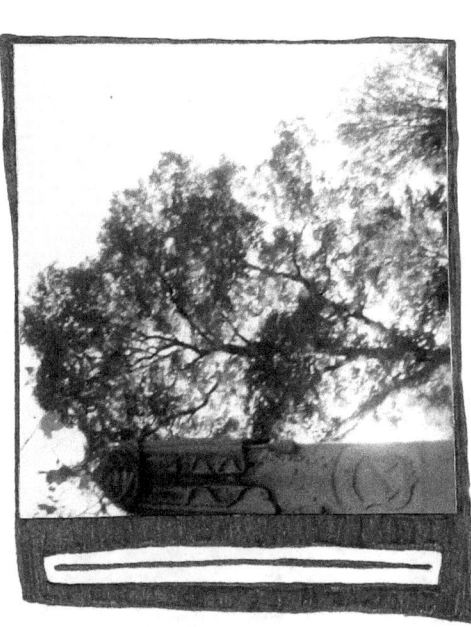

oh, hello there! You've come to the grand finale!

FIREWORKS.

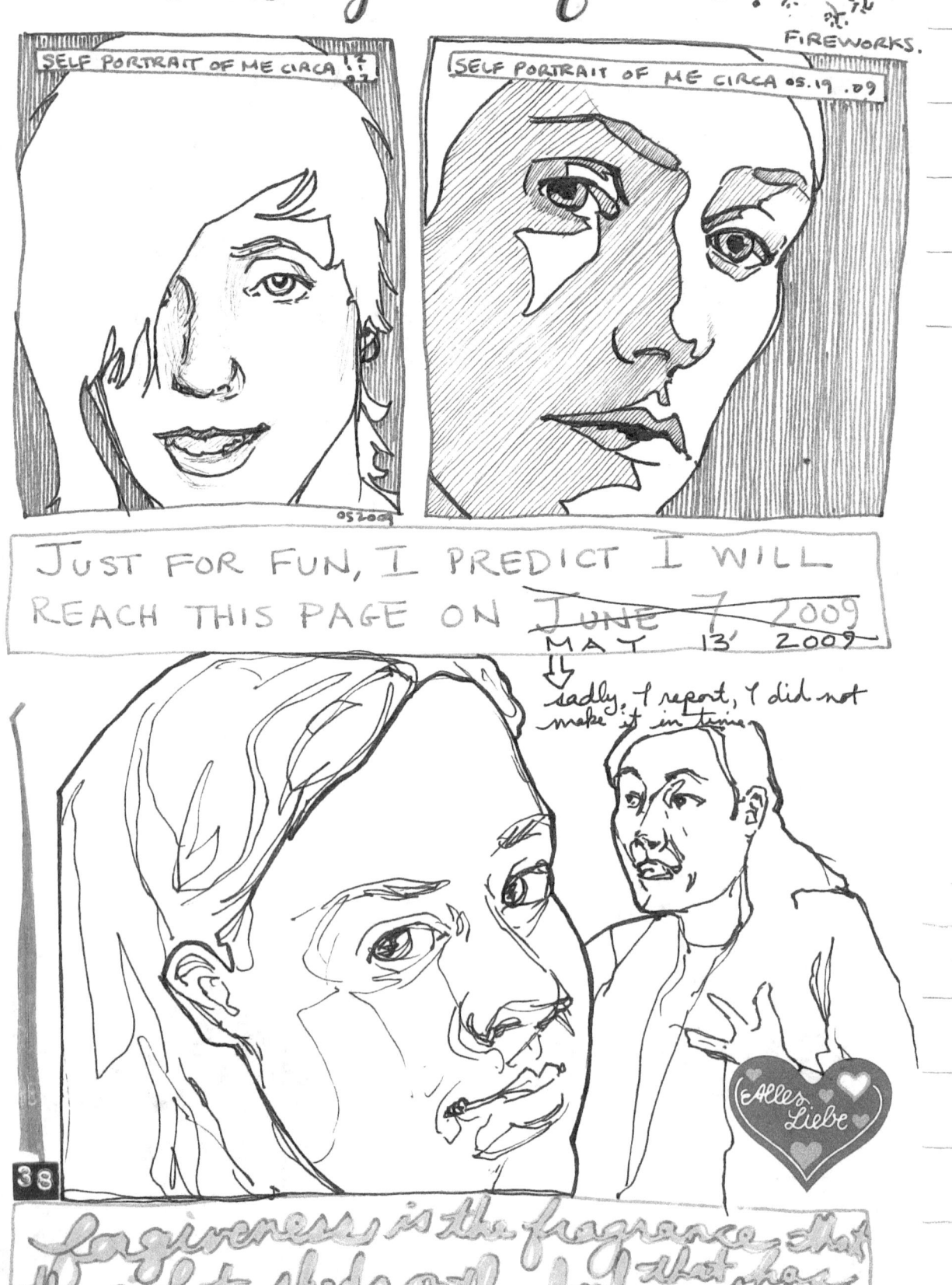

JUST FOR FUN, I PREDICT I WILL REACH THIS PAGE ON ~~JUNE 7 2009~~ MAY 13' 2009

sadly, I report, I did not make it in time

forgiveness is the fragrance that the violet sheds on the heel that has crushed it.

THANK YOU
⇩

JEFFREY - FOR THE
        CARTOGRAPHY LESSON
        ⇩

PORTLAND, OR - FOR THE
        SECOND CHANCE

∘——————————————∘

www.ingramcontent.com/pod-product-compliance
Lightning Source LLC
Chambersburg PA
CBHW060012210526
45170CB00017B/2317